BACKSTAGE BLACKOUT

The Diary of a Stage Tyrant

Philip Ronzone

authorHOUSE®

AuthorHouse™
1663 Liberty Drive
Bloomington, IN 47403
www.authorhouse.com
Phone: 1 (800) 839-8640

Published by AuthorHouse 08/10/2017

ISBN: 978-1-5462-0236-3 (sc)
ISBN: 978-1-5462-0234-9 (hc)
ISBN: 978-1-5462-0235-6 (e)

Library of Congress Control Number: 2017911868

Print information available on the last page.

Any people depicted in stock imagery provided by Thinkstock are models,
and such images are being used for illustrative purposes only.
Certain stock imagery © Thinkstock.

This book is printed on acid-free paper.

DEDICATION

N ow to the "Thank You", "I could not have done it without your part of this book".

The problem with giving thanks is that someone is usually left out.

The one person, above all others is my wife, Tomijean, of thirty-five years who contacted AuthorHouse. Tomijean is the greatest. Everything good in my life, today, has Tomijean's DNA on it. If not for her, there would be no book.

Next is my sister Roslie or Rhodie as I have always called her. Raised Catholic, then growing into a fine Christian woman, she was exposed to "This thing" also known as the book. Rhodie transferred a written text on to an outdated computer platform, a floppy disk. Tomijean restored the floppy disk to life, after it sat silently for fifteen years.

Thank you to Sir Bill Overman who talked to me for two years before any formal action on this book was started.

Thank you to Dan Tuziak for his technical support.

It was never my intent to put this text into book form. I actually wrote the book for my daughter Doriane. I guess I did not realize that Doriane would not be able to read this text until she was much older.

INTRODUCTION

Everything, with perhaps one exception, has a beginning and an end.

This book is no different.

At the time I wrote this, I was a card carrying member of IATSE, Local #720. (I think I know what all the big letters mean but I'm not sure).

In 2008, I retired from IATSE local #720. Stagehands, boy I fit right in. Sadly many of my co-workers and friends have passed away.

Yes, we were crazy. Even destructive in our personal behavior. Yes, we probably took our pranks and jokes too far. But I'll tell you this; I worked with a great bunch of men and women. Even animals!

We had some really intelligent people. People who worked with their hands. Such as Carpenters, Painters, Prop people, Electric, and Sound.

The best show is one where you see great talent and great sound and lighting.

When the show is over, you look to your partner and say "WOW, I can't believe it's over", or "WOW, I never have seen a stage set like that"!

If you haven't worked backstage or on a movie set, you really can't appreciate all the effort that goes into producing a product that is spectacular or a show that you will always remember.

I can honestly say that I had a job I loved. It never seemed like work. If I had to do it all over again, I would. Well most of it anyway.

Through the publishing process, I realized that so much more happened that I could tell. Maybe someday I will!

Yours Truly,
A Stage Tyrant

Contents

CHAPTER 1

WHERE DID THIS BOOK COME FROM?

Every once in a while I like to get a sheet of paper, a couple of pencils, and just write down whatever pops into my head. I haven't done this for quite a while, so let's see what happens.

What immediately comes to mind is that this is a terrible time to do this. It's during a part of the show in which I could easily miss a very important cue. No one likes to miss any stage cue. Funny things happen when people miss cues.

For instance, many times we'll be training new people, so if someone who should know better misses a cue, he just blames it on the new guy. It's a beautiful thing; however, once in a great while, the new guy has been paying attention and right when you're talking to the big boss, Mr. "I'm a New Guy Who Happens to Be Paying Attention" will say, "Hey, I didn't make any mistake; it was that guy." And when he points at me, well, that just sucks. Okay, I did it, can't blame a guy for trying. Most of the time though, the new ones will say, "Sorry," or, "I thought I was doing the right thing," and some of the less bright ones are good for a lot of mileage. Do we feel bad? Of course not; we just wish we had been as smart as Mr. Paying Attention New Guy when the other guys had done it to us.

My old boss was a special piece of work. When I first met him he told me I was too pretty to be a stage carpenter or prop guy, so the next night I was instructed to start on "the rail." All those bastard's who just let me be sacrificed that night were burned into my mind forever, and one by one I hunted them down and got even.

Of course at the time I thought I had just hit the lottery. Dion, the boss, seemed like a cool cat, which he was—until you missed a cue.

Missing a cue or performing the wrong cue on Dion's crew was an event that you never forgot. After the mistake, Dion would let everyone know that you would answer to a new name, at least for a while. Let me see if I can remember some of my old stage names. My favorite: "Shit for Brains". First runner up: "Cock-Sucking Idiot". Let's not forget "Dumb Cock-Sucker." Some guys, myself included, were too dumb, too thick-skinned, or just too loaded to take it personally. Others were not so fortunate.

The trick was to shut up, make no excuses…oh—and answer to your new name. There were the guys, however, who didn't know the trick. These poor bastard's would make the first mistake; then, either during their verbal reaming or shortly afterwards, would make a second or third mistake and do it all in a matter of minutes. You wouldn't think that Dion could reach new levels of nicknames for people, but that was the thing about Dion. He was always full of surprises.

Some men walked out, ruined; many vowed never to come back. Some were told politely that they shouldn't count on coming back; others were told not so politely.

Ah, but those who made it were a special breed. If you could make it here, you could make it anywhere. The odd thing is, Dion was a really good friend and there isn't a day that goes by that I don't think about him or find myself letting out a little chuckle at some memory of my friend, "The Pineapple Princess".

There is one scenario of cue malfunction that should not be overlooked, and that is the "Maybe Nobody Saw It" cue mishap. Normally, nine times out of ten, a person gets lucky and nobody did see anything. But then something happens—perhaps because the person feels guilt or has a deep sense of truthfulness, although I believe it's because they are relieved to think they really got away with something. However, after they get away with this big mistake, which no one else knows about but them, they will turn around and tell the guy next to them all about it and in five minutes everyone, including the CEO of the hotel, knows about it.

It's strange what road a wandering mind can travel; maybe the saying about a mind being a terrible thing to waste is not all it's cracked up to be. Perhaps a few could be wasted and they would be none the worse for wear.

Actually, I've found that almost everyone and everything has a purpose, myself included. Who knew or would have ventured to guess what the future would bring? And about that future...on second thought, the future looks a little scary. That leaves us two choices, the past or today. Perhaps there are more choices, but I probably wouldn't know about them anyway.

The past it is—and thank the good Lord I can remember parts if it. What's nice is talking to the old timers. Old timers are the people who have more than my 27 years in this business. Times change, everything changes, but I'd like to believe that there are memories and people and events that were not only funny but also downright hilarious. The people were no less than legends, some even icons, in the Hall of Fame of Stagehand. If there is no such institution, then there sure as hell should be.

Stagehand—you could ask ten people on the street, "What is a stagehand?" I'd bet they would all say about the same thing. But if you asked those same people what exactly is it that Stagehand do, the answers could be profoundly diverse.

It's no big secret that this business is often passed down from father to son; often aunts, uncles, nephews, and whole families can be involved. But like most things in my life, my introduction to the wonderful world of Stagehand did not take place in the usual way; in fact, I did not even know this business existed.

I had a job driving around town in an ambulance, smoking pot, taking all the acid I could shove in my mouth, and picking up drunks and dead babies. Actually, I was having a pretty good time.

One day I moved into a townhouse owned by my cousin, who had to follow her job to a different city. Less than a month later I met a gentleman who lived across the street. Ray was a spotlight operator at a small hotel on the strip; I'd seen him leave for work and it seemed that only a couple of hours later, he'd be back home.

I remember it was a Thursday night, Ray's birthday in fact, and he came over to invite me to come to work with him. What the hell, I had nothing better to do. Throughout the night as I watched Ray work I kept thinking, "Hey, this is really cool; I could do this." If he even hinted at the possibility of bringing me into this business, I'd jump at it.

No sooner had I run those thoughts through my mind when Ray said, "How would you like to run a spotlight?" Well Ray, I don't know, right now I'm working 48 hours on shift, 48 off, making a third of the money you do, and—holy shit, was that a naked girl I just saw? Okay, I'm in.

When I first started working at a showroom as a regular employee, I just couldn't believe that I was in the stage business. When family or friends would ask me about my new job I felt like a big shot. "Yes, I work backstage at the such-and-such show." It was so glamorous. Later, five or ten years down the road, I remember someone asking me about my job and I told him something like, "Well, I play cards, drink beer, and watch naked women." Finally I was expressing myself like a true stagehand.

So there I was at the Holiday Casino, training six or seven days a week. I did two shows a night and three shows on Fridays and Saturdays.

Little did I know how much Ray and his partner loved me. At first when Ray felt confident that I knew the cues he would tell me, "Phil, I'm gonna go down and grab a Coke." It turned out that he always talked in code. What he really meant was that he'd be right back after he did a huge line of cocaine. I was wondering how this guy stayed awake during the third show on the weekends, since I was sure having a hard time.

It didn't take me long to catch on. Clue number one: Ray never came back with a Coke. He always came back with a couple of double Cheval Reals. Clue number two: it's really hard to get the smell of weed off your clothes, especially when you still have half a joint in your pocket.

By the third week I was feeling a little bit upset. Hey, I wanna get a Coke too! Then one night I noticed that Ray had a handful of $25 poker chips in his hands. My mind was racing and panic ran through my veins. "Could he actually have been gambling while I was working the show?" I asked myself.

Now I don't know if I mentioned it or not, but because I was learning I wasn't getting paid. I reminded myself that here was a guy who picked me, out of all the people he knew, to do something really nice for. It was a great career change, and this particular line of work was hard to get into. "Just be thankful," I said to myself. But the fact of the matter was that I was feeling left out. There was some major partying going on and I wasn't included.

Then one night, when I thought Ray couldn't possibly pull any more shit, he did. He left me as usual right after the show began, only this time he was gone longer than normal. Shit, that's just great—here I'm working, the other guy gets the pay, gets totally whacked out and gets to gamble or whatever. Be grateful? Grateful really sucks.

Finally Ray returned and with him was one of the prettiest blonde ladies that I have ever seen. Now that's more like it! I was really taking a good look at this lady. Meanwhile, the comedian who was on stage at the time was saying, "Hey buddy, do you think I can have some light down here?" What was that? Did somebody say something? It doesn't matter.

Pam (this was the blonde's name) was just about to undo the last of the buttons on her cute little cotton blouse. This was great; this was fantastic!

"Come on guys, I need a little light down here."

Pam had a really nice set of tits, really shaped nice, full and natural, as best as I could tell. And the nipples...this time I was sure I heard something. Someone was talking...I tuned in.

"...Some goddamn..." Wow, it sounded like somebody was really pissed. "...LIGHT!"

HO FUCK, it's the comic, and right about now nobody is laughing.

The light coming out of my follow spot was not on the comic in a full body position. My light was not even on the stage. In fact, in the heat of passion, my light somehow ended up—or should I say down—in about, oh, the fourth or fifth row of the audience, where the new stars of the show turned out to be an elderly couple of about eighty.

This could only be described as a major fuck-up, and not used to being in such a situation, I had to take quick and decisive action. Above all I needed to keep a cool head.

What actually happened is that, under my control, the light jerked up from the audience, traveled all over the downstage area, lit up part of the upstage area, continued all the way up to the ceiling, dropped back down to the stage deck once again, and finally settled on the comedian.

The whole thing took maybe twenty seconds, but sometimes that seems like a lifetime. I'll never forget what Ray said to me. "Phil, I think you're ready to move on." I panicked because I thought he meant I wasn't going to be in the entertainment business any more. But that wasn't the case. Ray took me over to the lounge at the International Hilton where I "broke in" (worked for free) for another month, and then got my first call out of the Union.

CHAPTER 2

THE REAL DEAL

My first official call out of the Union was to report to the main showroom at the Hilton Hotel. I was to replace someone who was taking some time off.

Actually, two of us were out of the "Hall" that night. The other guy was an old timer who seemed to know everyone, while I knew no one. This place was huge; in fact, it's no lie, I got lost twice just trying to find the light booth.

When I did find the booth, the Head Electrician introduced himself and showed me the spotlight I was to operate that night. That's the first time the phrase "take my breath away" had meaning for me. Where's the stage? I wondered.

"Did you say something?" asked Kenny, the head electrician.

"No," I answered. I was starting to feel a little sick. Looking down over the edge of that light booth gave me the feeling that I could fall right through the window and into the audience. In the end everything worked out, but I did hear a funny story while I was there. I don't know if it's true, but here goes.

Evidently, a couple of weeks before I showed up at the Hilton, some person was dispatched from the Hall to run a spotlight for a couple of nights. The first night he showed up, but by the time he did his paperwork, attended to his light and all, he had no time left to eat. As he was sitting there at the spotlight a couple of minutes before the show started, he noticed a bowl of peanuts.

This was too good to be true; it was like a starving man on a desert island finding a coconut. These were the best tasting peanuts he had ever eaten, far better than any ballpark peanuts. It wasn't too long before the bowl was almost empty. He thought, "I really should leave a few." But in the end, he gobbled them all down.

The next night he brought in a big bag of peanuts and as he walked up to the spotlight, he saw an old man sitting there.

"Excuse me," the young man said. "I brought you a bag of peanuts to replace what I ate last night. It's just that I was so hungry I couldn't help myself."

There was a strange glint on the old man's eyes. Then a big smile broke out and the old man said, "Well, that's quite all right. Don't think I'm not grateful, but I only buy chocolate-covered peanuts, because with my bad gums and all, I don't actually eat the peanuts. I just suck the chocolate off of them and put them back in the bowl."

Well, that was the story.

I was "on the bounce", the term used for someone who doesn't have a steady job but works just about anywhere there is work. It was a lot of fun back then, and I met a lot of people. Some are still good friends today.

By the time I walked into the Tropicana I had already been at quite a few places: Union Plaza, Caesar's Palace, the Dunes, Holiday Casino, the International Hilton, the Flamingo Hilton, the Sahara, the Hacienda, and a few others I've probably forgotten about.

It was the Tropicana that would be my home for the next 25 years. It was also at the Trop that I would experience life, death, and the adventures and situations that prompted me to write this. It wasn't really my idea; over the years, I've been told time and time again that I should write these things down. Imagine my surprise to find out that this writing shit is not all that easy.

Let me first say that there were a few funny things that did happen before I adopted the Trop.

One not-so-funny thing that happened was an electric-work call I took at Caesar's. I was very new to stagehand work, and on this particular day I was told to go to the grid (a very high ceiling) and assist another fellow who was repairing some cable. Specifically, he was replacing some burnt pin connectors.

I had left most of my tools on the deck and was carrying just a crescent wrench and a couple of screwdrivers in my pocket. We had been working for about fifteen minutes or so when I stood up and a piece of wire or something snagged the Phillips head screwdriver in my back pocket. Before I could grab it, down it went through the ribbon steel of the grid floor, seventy or eighty feet to the deck below. I didn't do one right thing—no "Heads up on the deck!" No warning. Nothing.

Still, I was not done being stupid yet. Right after I heard it hit I started to yell, "Hey, would somebody grab that…"

The next thing I heard was "Shut the fuck UP. NOW!" I thought, how dare he talk to me like that? What was the big deal?

After five minutes of guidance and a severe lecture, I knew what was wrong. We finished our job and went back down to the deck. I took a couple of minutes to walk over to the part of the deck we had been working over, to see if I could find the screwdriver. There were a bunch of road boxes and piles of cable all around. Finally I found it. The screwdriver had pierced a section of 50-amp cable; its tip was buried in the wooden deck, three quarters of an inch to one inch deep. No doubt it could have killed somebody. I just left it there. To this day, I know I should probably be more cautious when working high. Well, some of us are slow learners.

Another thing that was funny (I guess it depends on your point of view) happened while I was at the Sands. I was what they called a "B-Lister", which meant I wasn't in a secure position. A person who was an "A-Lister" could bump me for my job. This is a practice you don't see happen too often, but it does happen.

I'd been working at the Sands for about two and a half months and the job was fantastic. The sound department had it made. All I did was stand in the wing stage right, and as the entertainer prepared to go on stage, I would hand him or her the microphone; then I would have to watch the cable so the entertainer wouldn't have a big mess or get tangled up in the thing. That was it. I met the likes of Don Pickles,

Rich Little, Bob Newhart, and a host of others. Every night for just a few minutes I would talk and kid around with these guys before they went on stage. Cool!

Then one day a fellow by the name of Michael T. came along. He had a habit of drinking a little too much before work, so he didn't do too well on the follow spot. Props seemed to baffle him a bit too much. My job, however, seemed to appeal to Mike greatly. The day he suggested that a stool for me to sit on would definitely make my job easier, was the day I knew I was in trouble.

Sure enough, two days later, the head soundman came up to me and gave me the bad news. An "A-Lister" had bumped me for my job. I was pissed—that was six hundred and fifty dollars a week take-home pay that I had just gotten fucked out of. Plus, I was just a month or two from getting my union card and being placed on the "A" list.

Every Friday was payday, and we would go up to the light booth to receive our checks. To get there you'd have to go up a small stairway, through a small conference room and into the booth. Along the same wall as the booth door was a section of drape twenty feet long, extending from ceiling to floor. It was about 15 inches from the wall, so you could walk between the drape and the wall.

I was just inside the conference room when I saw a movement behind the drapes. I quietly walked forward and soon I could hear the low sound of voices.

"Yeah, I just snagged me a killer job from that dumb shit kid." He couldn't be talking about me, could he? To this day I don't know who the other person was, but they were somehow connected to the Entertainment Department.

I heard the other guy say something like, "Hey, is that why you're in the Union, so nobody can fuck you? Besides, it's better to fuck them first." No, I hadn't fucked him, but I was getting ready to.

I stepped closer and figured out their position. Every once in a while the curtain would bulge out a little or move when they touched it.

Now, it's a fact that I was pretty well pissed off with the whole situation, and now behind Curtain Number One was the object of my anger. There was just one small problem—which person was which? A fifty-fifty chance…hey, I'll take those odds.

The only light in the room was one of those fluorescent jobs; I reached up and twisted one out, which made the lights flicker. Then the other tube fell out; the room went dark except for the light spilling out from the light booth.

Now the two guys were quiet. Time was running out; it was now or never. There—a movement. I kicked the hump in the curtain pretty hard, right where I thought their shins were.

"Jesus, Mike! What did I do? My leg hurts like hell." Sorry, so much for those fifty-fifty odds. Well, he deserved it just for being with that asshole. I kicked again and punched the curtain hard, about chest level. I was rewarded with a short sigh, the sound of air being knocked out of someone.

"My God!" It was Mike talking. "You got the wrong guys. Jesus, man, stop!"

Like hell I'll stop. A couple more well placed kicks and I'm outta here. True to my word I kicked away. The last one hit just the curtain, and I fell right on my ass. I got out of there.

It's funny how something happens and then later you hear quite a bit different story. While picking up my final paycheck, I saw Mike in the booth talking about what had happened. I came in a little late during the conversation, but it went something like this:

Mike was saying he'd met his friend, who also worked at the Sands (but not as a stagehand), right outside the light booth. Mike was going to loan his friend some money to pay a gambling debt. Some collection guys followed the friend and caught up with him as he met Mike. Before they knew it, Mike and his buddy were in a war zone. Mike said there were at least two, more likely three or four big fuckers beating the shit out of them. Fortunately, something scared the guys and they left, but not before Mike got in some good shots.

I could see just the tail end of a black eye on Mike. He must have been lying on the ground or something. I picked up my check, said goodbye to all the fellows and moved to Brian Head, Utah, for the winter.

CHAPTER 3

ASSAULT ON THE ZOO

My winter in Brian Head was, to this day, the best time of my life, but as happens to all good things, it came to an end. So I packed up my truck and headed back to Vegas. I'd almost quit the stage business, but I ran into Ray again and he persuaded me to sign in again with the Union.

Once again, I was on the bounce. I've heard lots of guys complain that they never get enough work while bouncing. I liked the bounce; I met a lot of people and every job was different. Some were far better paying than a weekly house job paycheck. I never seemed to get any time off. Between Caesar's, the Riviera and the Sands, I never starved. In fact, I made a very decent living.

Then in March of 1976 I was told by dispatch to report to the Head Carpenter for the Follies Bergere show at the Tropicana. This was the beginning of a whole chapter—no, change that—many chapters of my life. This is where the real story begins. This is no soap opera; these characters are real. If I'm not mistaken, I referred to some of them earlier as legends.

There was life lived to the fullest, fast times, and hard living. There was also death. I don't know of many lessons I learned, or if we were supposed to learn any. It was a party.

As I walked onto the stage of the Folies, I had the usual feelings of anxiety—new cues, that sort of thing. I asked a couple of guys where I might find Pat, but nobody could seem to find him.

The announcement, "Fifteen minutes!" had just sounded when this little guy came around the corner with a drink in one hand and a cigarette in the other.

"Are you Pat?" I asked. "I'm supposed to report to Pat."

He just looked at me for a moment and then said, "Yeah, I'm Pat. H-h-h-how ya doing, darling fu-fu-fu-fuck?"

I gotta tell you, this took me by surprise. First of all, I thought, I'm not your darling fuck. Second: who was this guy? The boss, that's who. Oh well, he was partying, so he couldn't be all that bad.

The guys stage right were all older than I was, but they were nice and helped me through the first show. Then, right before the second show started, I was standing by Pat when this big guy (well, he looked big to me) came up to Pat and pointed at me. "That boy is dressed too pretty. Also looks like he could pull ropes. I think he'd be better on the rail."

No way, what's a rail anyway? I didn't know, but I didn't like the sound of it. Pat said something like, "Sure, Pa-Pa-Pa-Princess." Oh thanks, way to sell me down the river. I could have been a great prop guy, maybe one of the best.

Now I was going to be on the rail. Now I was going to work for this tall—and, as guys would put it—somewhat good-looking Hawaiian guy who struck me as being arrogant as hell. There are events in our lives that are landmarks, turning points if you will; sometimes they are traumatic and sometimes, like this one, they pass without our knowing.

This was a huge event. Who would have known that I would work the rail from that day until now, at least 25 years and counting? Who could have predicted the friendships that would be forged over the next quarter-century? As life went on, there were friends I would lose. I lived two or three lifetimes during those years.

Going back to the start of the Trop years, I have to introduce Dion, AKA "The Pineapple Princess"—at least that was his most famous nickname. I, however, had a few others for him over the years. Dion was the gentleman who recruited me for the rail, so the following evening I came to work and reported to the rail.

As I walked across the stage I could see several people sitting around a card table. The closer I got, I was sure of one thing—actually, a couple of things. First of all, these guys were young, not like the guys stage right. Another thing I noticed was that a couple of these guys were almost as tall sitting down as I was standing up. They wore beards, long sideburns, and almost everyone had long hair. These guys looked like they liked to party. My kind of guys.

I walked up close to the table but stopped a few feet away. They were playing cards and I didn't want to bother them, so I waited until the hand was over. During that time I sized them up a little more. I was right, these guys were big, and the smaller ones were stocky and strong looking. Not only that, they didn't look all that friendly.

"What do you want?"

What a nice greeting, and how do you do? But what I said was, "Hi. Dion told me to come to the rail; is he here?"

"Yeah," was the answer, and that was about it. So I sat down and waited. As the intercom announced, "Half hour, thirty minutes", Dion came walking over.

"Come here," Dion said. "This is Tom; he'll show you what to do. Have you ever worked on a rail before?"

Shit, I don't know why, but that was the question I was hoping wouldn't be asked. Perhaps it's because I really wanted a full time job, or maybe I didn't want to appear uneducated in the field of stage work, but I answered so quickly that once the words were out of my mouth, it was too late.

"Yes, I've worked on a rail before, at Bally's Hallelujah Hollywood." This was technically true, for I had worked the rail one night.

"Okay, that's good; Tom, you teach him."

Whew, glad that's over; now all I needed was to watch these guys for the first show and then I was pretty sure I could fake my way through this thing. I did know "back line out, front line in", but that was about it, and even that I had to stop and think about.

Finally the show started and Big Tom (and I do mean big—six feet, four or five inches and all of 280 pounds) got up and told me, "Put your gloves on and stand by line 59. On the blackout, fly it—fast.

Then stand by 55 leg. After the gazebo clears, bring it in, then bring in 45. I'll give you a stand by, then a go. Got it?"

Whoa, whoa, whoa! Wait a minute, Tom, could you slow down a minute and repeat that...

"Standby, GO!"

I'm in big trouble. Did you say...

"Go, asshole!"

Christ, you're hurting my ears...

"Back line! Pull the back line. Okay, okay, don't get so upset. Faster. Move it! You should have 55 half way in by now."

Hey, I can go faster...There are few sounds louder on stage than an arbor with fifteen hundred pounds of pig iron smashing into the end of the track, or stopping point—the end of the line. Well, you get the picture; if you don't, here's a brief description.

The arbor slides along a track; on the Folies rail, these tracks are seventy to eighty feet long, or actually, high, because they run vertical to the stage floor. The iron sits on these arbors.

Now I'm not sure how fast a man can pull this weight in or out, but the arbors move pretty quickly. Starting the process is only part of the action. You also have to stop the arbors. Imagine that! So when all that weight, traveling at, say, ten to fifteen miles per hour, smashes into a metal and wood stop, well, it makes a very loud noise. A lot like an auto wreck.

If you also add the fact that it's happening during a set change, it just stands to reason that there is no music playing for a couple of seconds—and that's when you hear it. The whole rail hears the crash; all of stage right hears; the poor bastard in the farthest seats from the stage, all the way in the back of the audience, can hear. Hell, it would be a miracle if the hotel across the street wouldn't call up and ask which room tower just fell down. It's that loud.

Tom was fit to be tied right about then. What else could go wrong? Well, I'll tell you.

There are black curtain "legs", designed to block the audience's view into the stage wings (offstage areas). The legs are soft pieces, so you could have a hard time telling exactly when they touch the stage;

that's why Stagehand put little pieces of red gaffer's tape on the line, so you know when to stop pulling and engage the lock. However, if one does not know what the tape is for—well, the end result is that the curtain piles up on the deck.

Now I had Tom screaming at me to take out 45, back out to the trim mark. Okay, now I'm starting to understand. Hey, look at me! Too bad Tom wasn't joining me in my celebration. As a matter of fact he was downright pissed. "All right, so I'm a little rusty," I said. "It could have been worse, couldn't it?"

Tom still hadn't said anything. Then Dion came up rail and that's the first time I saw him in action. "Hey, Shit for Brains," he said to Tom. "I thought you were watching that guy. If your brains were shit you wouldn't know where to wipe! Dumb cocksucker."

Poor Tom, probably one of the nicest guys ever to walk the earth, and for twenty years he remained Dion's favorite person to pick on.

Believe me, all of us on the rail were often reminded that we were pretty fucking bad excuses for Stagehand, and the one thing we did all have in common was "Shit for Brains."

If you could work for Dion, you could work for anyone. I can remember quite a few guys walking out after the second show, mumbling things like, "That son of a bitch, I'll never take another call for the rail at the Trop, never." And they would tell their friends. Others walked out almost in tears. The scary ones were the silent ones with murder in their eyes; yeah, you felt you had to watch out for those guys. They might come back and put a cap in your ass.

The thing about Dion was, he never stayed mad for long. He could ride you all night long, call you every name you ever dreamed of, make you feel like he hated you more than anything on this earth, you low life. But the next day he'd be over at your house with his bobcat tractor, moving dirt, or helping you add on to your house—whatever. I think he did everything in his power to hide the fact that he was a nice guy, that he had a heart of gold.

I remember a couple of years ago, sitting in the church at his funeral, I was looking around and there wasn't an empty seat in the whole place. People were standing all along the rear of the church and into the lobby; there were even a few people outside the church. A couple of people told me they couldn't bear to attend the service. I knew how they felt. I couldn't help but cry—the first time in many years.

On the casket were several photographs. I remember two in particular. One was Dion on his Harley Davidson motorcycle, which he took great pains to conceal from his wife, for what reason I'm not sure. I guess she was one of the few people he didn't want to tangle with.

The second photo was of Dion and his wife, Audrey, on their wedding day. This guy had movie star good looks in his youth. No kidding; this man should have, and probably could have, been a movie star. I guess the way you'd describe Dion was: he was a man's man. He was such a character and truly one of the legends, still referred to in conversations around this stage and many others.

Nothing like getting sidetracked…Meanwhile, going back to Tom…

When he finally did speak to me, he was actually very calm. Extremely calm for someone who just went through a royal reaming. In a very controlled voice, he said, "I don't like people who don't tell the truth. They're called liars. If you ever lie to me again I'll beat the shit out of you." He could have done it, too.

Tom was very patient, and in no time at all I learned the set of cues. Dion then had me learning all the rail cues, five sets in all.

As time went on it became my opinion that the rail was, without a doubt, the best place to work on the stage. For one thing, we were somewhat isolated from everyone else, which was a blessing for those other people. Also, with the exception of Dion, everyone else was in their mid-twenties and we all liked to party. It seemed that everyone on stage right were drinkers, everyone on stage left were dopers and drinkers. A very explosive mix at the time—very explosive indeed.

CHAPTER 4

KIDS—PLAY NICE!

Most people get up in the mornings, do whatever their daily routine is, then off they go to a job they really do not like; for some, it's a job they hate. Me, it was just the opposite. I've talked to several guys and we all agree: work was where we went to get high and party; it's where the wild girls were, the naked girls. Oh sure, we actually had things to do every once in a while, but there was plenty of time to get into trouble.

I was pretty lucky because most of these guys had been working together for a while and they were a very tight group. However, I was a match made in heaven for this group, sort of the missing piece of the puzzle. After I joined the rail crew, it stayed the same for many years. It was like a marriage, until death do us part.

It's kind of hard to know where to begin, partly because we're talking twenty, twenty-five years ago. For the most part we all got along pretty well, considering the diversity of the crew. However, I do recall in particular one ongoing feud between two crewmembers.

Big Tom and Herb Hull seemed to have some bad blood between them, and it had been going on for some time before I got there.

One night it finally happened. During the show we had one set change that seemed dangerous. Two large set pieces would enter onto the stage, one from stage right and the other from stage left. On each offstage end were stairways that went up fifteen feet or so. These two pieces were secured in place using stage pins. At that point, Tom had to lower in a line that held a sandbag on it. The purpose of the sandbag was to put some weight on the line; without weight you could take the line out, but you couldn't bring it back in.

As Tom was lowering the bag in, the person on the deck was putting the pin in, and then would grab the bag as it landed on the deck. Unhooking the bag, he would then use the snap hook to attach the line to an eyebolt on the set piece; this process was done to both set pieces at the same time. When that was done, two fly men (rail crew), each pulling on different lines, would lift the part of the set that was hinged. When in place and secured, the two set pieces were linked together, forming a high arch or bridge that the performers would walk across or stand on, depending on what their position called for. Basically, it was a long walkway fifteen feet high, about five feet wide, and about forty feet long with steps on each end.

In their respective positions, Tom controlled the sandbag and Herb was the pin man who unhooked the bag. You have to understand that this setup took place in a pretty short amount of time; also, it was pretty dark on stage.

I'd see Tom leaning over the pin rail, looking out over the stage and lowering the sandbag. I guess because he'd done it so many times, he had made a little game of it. He'd lower the bag so that when Herb would stand up after putting the pin in place, it would just barely clear his head. Like I said, we partied a lot and back then, we had an hour and forty-five minutes between shows. That's ample time to smoke a joint or two, down three or four double scotch and waters, eat another Quaalude, and go back for the second show. Now I'm not saying that's what Tom did; I was speaking for myself. But whatever he did, his vision or perspective was a little off, because every once in a while Herb would stand up and hit his head on the bag.

This would really get Herb mad; at times you could hear him screaming at that "cocksucker" all the way across the stage. Even the music was no match for Herb.

On this particular night, Tom was lowering the sandbag, but halfway in, the rope slipped out of his hand and fell until it hit—you guessed it—Herb's head. Even though I couldn't see him, I knew the bag hit Herb. I thought, "Gee, Herb's taking it quite well. No screaming, no cursing, nothing."

A few seconds later I heard Tom say, "Shit." As I looked out to the stage I saw Herb get up on one knee and realized that Tom had knocked Herb flat out on the deck. This was bad news. I had heard rumors that some of the guys packed weapons from time to time, and that Herb was one of them.

When Herb was all the way up, he turned toward the rail and started to trot over. See ya Tom, I'm outta here—if you're wise you'll join me. Tom did one of the smartest things I'd ever seen him do: he hid.

Fortunately Herb got himself under control and finished up his cues, but several times that night he came hunting for Tom. Every time we'd see him coming, the whole crew vacated. I don't remember how many days we were worried, but in the end, somehow they worked it out.

Thank God we were all good friends, especially on the rail. It was not uncommon to see arguments almost come to blows, but at least one person usually had the sense to step in and cool things down. It seemed like everyone played peacemaker from time to time. Myself, I'm not the biggest guy, so it was kind of scary to get between two guys who were each six feet five and 250 pounds and plead with them not to beat the shit out of each other.

One time I actually started a fight just by making a fart noise. I was walking out of the stage area with a group of guys after the second show. Two of the people in the group had an ongoing personality conflict, for reasons that were a mystery to me, but the fact was that they just didn't care for each other.

I was bringing up the rear and there was a couple walking towards us, probably guests, and since I was in the rear, they really couldn't see me. I thought it would be really funny to make a farting sound just as they reached our group. At what I thought was the perfect time I made the loudest, most obnoxious fart sound that I could conjure up. Well, imagine my surprise when one guy in our group lunged at the other guy because he thought he'd been disrespected, or made fun of.

There they were, arms swinging, feet kicking, then they were rolling on the ground. One of the guys had a brother in the group, and this brother ran inside to get someone in Security. I'm not saying that this was the wrong thing to do, but I thought he might have tried to help his brother, stop the fight, anything, but he thought it best to get Security. We never did see this brother again that night. The fight broke up and we all went home; if he or Security came, we never saw them. The next night I apologized to both of them and we all laughed because it was a ridiculous thing.

Did I learn my lesson? No. Throughout the years I've been at the Follies show, fart sounds, especially loud farts, have been a constant source of laughter. And it wasn't just me; there have been some people who put me to shame.

One gentleman I worked with named Rob P. was the heavyweight champion, undisputed. Rob could clear out the rail faster than a bomb scare. What made Rob the master was that he had the ability that separates the men from the boys. It seemed like he had an endless supply of deadly, toxic gas. Sure, I had a couple of killer farts a night, but after a couple of big blasts, I'd shot my wad. Not Rob. Man, he could keep them coming. I know you're dying to hear the details, and I'd be a mean man if I didn't give them to you.

We have a big fan that is hung about ten feet up in the air, all the way at the end of the rail. The air is pushed all the way down the rail; then it flows around the corner of a big set piece called the Shadow Box; then it dies out after that. But that was far enough.

Because the show is fast paced, certain areas are set aside so the cast can change costumes quickly and get right back on stage. These areas were used three times during the show, but only for a few minutes each time. Paying attention to detail, Rob did some serious research. Combined with exact calculation, he soon had the formula he was looking for. I watched him; I was impressed.

Rob figured that by standing at Point A, which was about mid-rail (see diagram below), he could fart just as the last dancer exiting the stage was heading for the quick-change area and he'd get them all. It took five to eight seconds for the fart to travel to Point B. When the fart reached Point B, it would be blossoming into its maximum lethal stinkage, or MLS. Two more seconds to round the corner and BOOM! One hundred percent killing zone. God, what a genius; no wonder we all held him in awe.

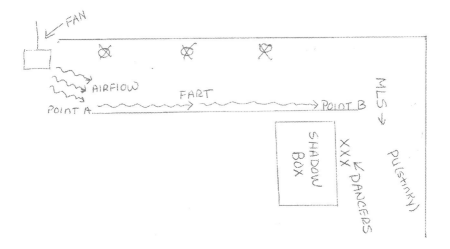

When Rob would let loose, we would all be quiet; you could hear the muffled chatter of the people who were changing their outfits—those poor innocent bastard who didn't stand a chance, trapped there until they had finished dressing.

The first person didn't even have time to sound an alarm; you'd hear pleas for mercy that went unanswered. "My God, that could make you puke and you'd consider yourself lucky." Rob's gas could render an adult helpless, even unconscious; a small child would die.

We all thought this was one of the funniest things we'd ever seen; even today, I think back and laugh. In all fairness, I'd have to tell you the down side.

During one of those quick changes, I and a couple of other unfortunate guys would have a cue to follow. If you would kindly refer once again to the diagram, you will notice three small circles with lines through them. These indicate our respective positions on the rail at the time we executed our cues. As you see, this was not a good thing; no, not good at all. I did not use the word "execute" by mistake, because that's what it was—an execution.

A wave of panic, followed by the overwhelming urge to throw up; then the fleeting thought of suicide. Jim Jones and his followers, who all drank that Kool-Aid laced with poison and died, they were cowards. With Rob you knew what was coming and you couldn't move; worst of all, you didn't die.

And when you finally were able to get away, well, by then it really didn't matter. Your mind was in a state of confusion, your respiratory system failing; some even experienced loss of vision or double vision. It often took minutes just to talk again. Yep, it was all fun and games until it happened to you. Rob—a true icon in the Hall of Fame of Stagehand.

Another great opportunity to gas people presented itself one day. It was right after one of our show changes took place that we noticed that one of the new props had definite possibilities. The prop was designed to be a magic box six feet high and about four feet square. There was a divider, or false wall, in the middle. As we watched how it worked in the show, we learned that two acrobats would come running all the way over from one side of the stage and get in the box. Two more would come running over and get in the other side, and the box would go out on stage where it would sit for about two minutes before the acrobats would be revealed. The whole time that the box was on stage, the audience could see it, so the acrobats couldn't open the doors without ruining the illusion.

On closer inspection, we found that the box was really well constructed. The door seams were almost invisible and had a flange piece on one side of the door, so when they closed together it was almost airtight.

Yes, this had definite possibilities. The first step was to test it out. I went inside one day with a cigar, closed the doors and puffed away. Two minutes was all I could take; my eyes were watering and the smoke was starting to choke me. I got out, closed the doors and gulped in the fresh air.

This magic box was a gold mine. We could go in there, smoke half a joint, get back out, and a second after the door closed, you couldn't smell a thing. It became the place to go if you didn't have time to go out back and have a couple hits. Nothing good lasts forever, so when we made the mistake of using the box before the act, a couple of the acrobats went to the entertainment director and told him what they suspected. Under the careful questioning of the director, we crumbled. Yes, you got us; we were smoking pot in the magic box. No, it won't happen again; on that you have our word. He didn't say anything about cigars.

We decided that the squealing little acrobats would have to be punished. You know, send out a message: you don't snitch on the Stagehand; if you do, you pay the price. We decided that we'd do it on the second show before our day off. I was going to take a cigar in there and fill that box up with as much smoke as possible. And I was going to do it right before they got in.

Then someone said, "What about Rob?" Oh my God, Rob! Whoever came up with that suggestion should get the goddamn Pulitzer Prize. No more talk, it was a done deal.

We knew Rob would say yes, but according to human nature, we knew if we presented it to him as a challenge, he'd give it his best effort. Trying to tie up all the loose ends, we reminded Rob to be sure to eat all the right food groups or whatever he needed to do to achieve the maximum results.

Rob didn't let us down. Once again there were cries for help, followed by coughing and gag-heaving noises. I'm not sure, but I think the acrobats got out of the box before they were supposed to.

The first show after our night off, we were sitting around the card table when a little band of acrobats approached us; all they were missing was a little white flag. Time to surrender, the desperate act to preserve lives; an agreement was reached. Smoking pot in the box after it was used in the show was agreed to, but no more farts. All you have to do is know how to negotiate.

It's a funny thing: here I was twenty-odd years later talking with Rob's son, who now works here, and he was telling me about how his dad would be in the supermarket and let a big fart out, then go to the end of the aisle and wait to see who would walk through it. Adam, his boy, said for some reason it would usually be a poor old lady that would damn near fall over. He said it would be like watching a person who is having a seizure or some type of fit.

Adam also said that when he would be at home with his friends, Rob would be in the kitchen and they'd hear a great big "Pfhhh," then hear him giggle. Adam said, "We'd laugh until the smell reached us, then we'd have to open up the windows." Jeez, Rob, I can understand gassing Joe Blow on the street or even your working partners, but your own kids—well, that just doesn't make sense. You might have damaged their brains or something. Of course, proving it is a whole different matter.

As I said earlier, I certainly did my share of stinking, but I always like to make it appear as though the other guy did it.

We had the Hawaiian Tropics International Pageant on our stage and during the rehearsals, a group of guys was standing a little ways on stage admiring the girls, making small talk. That's the kind of situation that I look for. I was behind the guys, hidden in the curtain, and had to make a decision: will it be a high, tight squeaker fart, or a deep, flappy fart? I find I'm most successful with deep and flappy. Once again, I wasn't disappointed. You'd think someone goosed a skunk out there, and the guys all of a sudden didn't feel so cavalier.

Thank God for modern technology; over the span of my career I've seen great strides made in this industry. In the fields of lighting and audio-visual, this is especially true. The computer has allowed unbelievable things to happen. Computer-generated graphics and images have made special effects an art form.

These things have been really good for the entertainment field. However, it would be irresponsible of me not to mention the Remote Operated Fart Machine, my personal one. I owe thanks to Howard Stern for making the knowledge available to me through his broadcast. Thank you, thank you. I've had more fun with this thing than should be allowed. The remote feature is impressive. I'm not sure what distance it's capable of, but it's a long way, and it always works.

We have a small room backstage that has some cabinets and is home to our coffee maker. This is where I decided to try out my new toy. I set it behind the garbage can and then went some distance away and waited. People went in one at a time for a few minutes, so I had to be patient.

Finally I got my chance when two showgirls entered the room together. I couldn't have picked two better people if I'd tried. Showgirls are a different breed, and I'm not saying I don't like them, because I do; but they're cautious and sometimes that is mistaken for being stuck up. These two, however, had been here for a while; one had an English accent and the other French, if I had to guess. Both had the presence of sophistication. Stuck up.

One grabbed a cup and started pouring coffee, with the other one standing slightly behind her. I pressed the remote and heard a squeaky fart. I was laughing so hard I almost fell down. What surprised me was their reaction, which was—nothing. They acted like nothing happened. Well, I wasn't done yet, not by a long shot.

Then something happened that I could not have planned better, not in a thousand years. One of the girls dropped a packet of sugar, and was bending over to pick it up.

I should explain that these machines have a variety of fart noises, but being a new owner, I had no way of knowing what sound would come out next. One thing is for sure, I have excellent rhythm and my timing was impeccable.

Just as the showgirl was bent all the way over, I pressed the button. This time the noise was a low, deep fart sound, but at the very end was a little high squeaker fart, kind of like two farts. She jerked up and turned around; both girls faced each other. I only wish I could have heard what they said, but both were embarrassed and thought the other had done it. It was like each one was waiting for the other to offer an apology. After a moment both kind of smiled and went on with their business, but mine wasn't done yet.

Just as the first girl was halfway out the door, I pressed the button again. This third fart sound was what you'd expect to come out of a drunken bum sleeping off a binge. It was deep, loose and flappy.

The first girl at the door looked back and I knew what she was thinking. She knew it wasn't herself; she'd never do that, but that disgusting sound definitely came from the other girl standing by the garbage can stirring her coffee. Yeah, you, the one with the bad breeding and no manners, filthy bitch.

Meanwhile, the other girl looked back and you could see a confused, bewildered look on her face. She would never do anything as disgusting as that in public; hell, she didn't even do that at home unless she was alone. But damned if it didn't sound like it came from her. No, no, this couldn't be, this just wasn't happening. Oh God, this other bitch is going back to the dressing room and tell everyone that I'm a pig, and by the sound of my farts, I've got a big flappy butt hole. Oh my God, then somehow the word will get out and my boyfriend will hear and he'll think, "That's why she doesn't take it in the rear; she's loose as hell." And then he'll tell all his friends and I won't be able to get a date, unless it's with some degenerate stagehand. If I don't have any dates, the girls in the dressing room will start rumors that I'm a lesbian…I'll probably lose my…Oh, stop it! The worst that will happen is that you'll be known as the girl who farts in public.

It was the little grin she finally showed on her face that got me, you know, the one you get that says, "I know I look guilty but I swear to God I'm innocent." I personally thought it was really cute.

The important thing is to tell only the people you can trust, so they can enjoy the joke, too; and also, don't give away the machine's effectiveness by using it too often.

The coffee room was good for a day or two, but then I had to cool it for a while. I needed a new location, but the logistics and special requirements that had to be met in order to get the maximum enjoyment out of my new toy turned out to be somewhat challenging.

Sitting on my chair on the rail one day, I noticed that when the girls came offstage to change costumes, which they did several feet off the rail, there were a couple of short two-or-three-second breaks in the music where my machine would be able to be heard.

If there was one design flaw in my fart machine, it was in the volume; it could have been a little louder (perhaps in the future they'll design one with an aroma disc of some sort. Wouldn't that be cool?) I started to pay more attention to what was happening; like, for instance, the fact that every girl had to bend over a couple of times because their costumes were all laid out on the floor. Now all I needed were two things. One, I desperately needed those music breaks to happen when the girls were there; two, I needed a good hiding place for my machine.

As it turned out, everything fell into place and once again, I was in business.

I'm one of those people who can't keep a straight face; I like to laugh, so when I would do these pranks I'd have to get away so I wouldn't blow it.

It was time again for fun. The girls came running offstage; a minute later there was a music break and a big juicy fart. It happened time and time again. People, especially women, do the polite thing by pretending that nothing has happened…it must have been a squeaky caster (wheel) or something. It was the second one they couldn't ignore, especially when the girls were all bending over and there were bound to be one or two whose heads were close to someone else's butt. Being close didn't even matter; just having your head down there was enough.

At first I'd hear sounds like moans. When the third fart sounded it was like, "God, that was so gross." Or, "Jesus Christ, who did that?" Then there were the ones that just giggled.

In the end, though, it was the wardrobe girls (the women who dress the dancers, make sure that every performer has the right clothes for every number in the show, clean and repair costumes on a daily basis— quite a lot of work) who found my fart box after they started getting blamed for passing the gas. To this day, they have never returned it. That's okay, because I received many nights of enjoyment with my toy.

I remember one night I was sitting behind the prop box, which was the box I'd hidden my fart machine under, when the same music breaks came. When it was quiet, I ripped a huge fart and one of the girls said, "Oh, that's just one of those machines again."

Another girl replied, "Yeah, but they were never that loud."

I was thinking, "And they never smelled like this, either." I guess that's when the butt aroma hit, because for some reason I can't explain, they all were looking at me.

CHAPTER 5

SO YOU WANT TO PARTY?

As I reached the point where I knew my cues, I started to relax and take part in the fun and games. Like I said before, we looked forward to work; this was when the action began.

I had a routine developed whereby I would stop at the Seven-Eleven and pick up two large cans of beer and one small can. By the time I reached work, the last can was finished off. During the ride, I'd also smoke a joint.

No wonder backstage seemed like a mystical place; with that altered perspective, plus all the big sets, curtains, and the lighting, it definitely was a strange atmosphere.

Before the first show started, there was plenty of time to go across the street, grab another beer, then sit out back and relax for a few more minutes. Another joint was usually passed around.

A new show edition, or new look for the Follies, takes place about every four years. With every new edition there is a new, different amount of time a person has between cues. For years, we on the rail had a lot of time. Fifteen to eighteen minutes between cues was not uncommon. Flymen, the term used to describe the people who work on the rail, usually do their cues at the end of one scene and the beginning of the next. It wasn't very often that we did something during the number. There were also two or three specialty acts in our show, and those always ran fifteen to twenty minutes. With that much time, we had to find things to do to amuse ourselves. Of course there was always getting loaded, smoking another joint, doing some blow…you kind of needed some by that time because, with all the beer and pot, you started to get a little tired and there was still a long night ahead.

Playing cards was one way to pass the time. We had some vicious games of Eights. Dion would go out front and see one of the guys in the casino pit and they would give him cartons containing boxes of cards that they had marked as not to be used on the tables any more. In our hotel's case, they would punch a hole about half the diameter of a pencil through the center of the deck.

In one carton there were about fifteen decks, and Dion would come back with three or four cartons, so we should have cards for years to come. I was wrong.

We couldn't go a week, and sometimes not that long, without someone throwing a deck across the table, out on the stage floor, in the garbage, or just against the wall, in a fit of anger. So it soon became apparent to me that at that rate of expenditure, we'd be lucky not to run out in a couple of months.

Dion was one you had to watch; can you believe he cheated? Well, I didn't know it at the time, but Dion figured that if these guys wanted to get so fucked up and then try to play a good game of cards, they deserved to be cheated on. But the way he did it…

It would be time for us to get up to do our cues and Dion, who didn't have a set of cues, would sit there and just pick up our hands and look at them, then set them back down. Like I said, it's the way he did it, smooth, like it was the most natural thing in the world to do. Some people would tell him to stop dealing from the bottom of the deck, but I could never spot it. He really didn't have to cheat, because he was a damn good card player; he had no problem keeping track of the cards, something I could never do.

Though I don't play anymore, today the card games continue, and even though you don't see the cards flying all over the place any more, the games are just as heated. As the Head Flyman, I still have to caution the boys to play nice from time to time, or I'll take their cards away.

A friend of mine by the name of Ross, whom I spent much time with, taught me a dice game he called "Ten Thousand." It was a fun game and was made more so, it seemed, when drugs and alcohol were involved. I introduced this game backstage one year when we were getting kind of burned out with the cards. I won't explain the mechanics of the game, but as the name indicates, the first team to reach ten thousand points wins the game. We had played the game for about six months or so, and had some very exciting and heated dice games. Unlike the card games, it seemed like certain teams formed and seldom changed.

My good friend and partner, Bob D., was my teammate. We were good; in fact, we were great! If we were ahead, the others just never caught up. If we were behind, well, we were nicknamed "The Comeback Kings", and rightly so. We were also labeled "The Worst Winners", which also was a deserved name. After the losers would have to listen to our bullshit talk, we'd get up on our chairs and give each other high fives and tell each other how great we were. And most of the time we could back it up.

After one particular thrashing, the other team, after being subjected to an unusually cruel verbal attack, suggested that because we were the "Kings" and best ever, we should have no problem accepting a small wager of, say, a penny a point. A penny a point? We laughed; that was not even worth our time. Not only are you guys suck-ass amateurs, but you disrespect the "Dice Kings", and that offends the "Dice Gods", which Bob and I both knew existed because we had appealed to them personally many times.

Bob and I stood fast and refused to be taunted by these peasants, these fake, imitation dice players, until one day when not our feelings but our pride and honor were violated.

Bob H. and his partner, who had received that particular thrashing I spoke of earlier, went too far; yes, they crossed the line. They went way past the good-natured kidding that Bob D. and I were so famous for. They called us "Chicken Shit." The thing is, they had to do it in front of the other guys. So as you can see, we finally had to concede and accept the penny-a-point challenge from these two losers.

Now that money was on the line, we needed to set up some rules. No matter what, no fist fighting; based on their past behavior, they had shown signs of wanting to do physical damage to Bob or myself. After that, we couldn't think of any more good rules, so it was time to play.

We all agreed that the contest was to last two weeks and on the next payday we would settle up. One of the last things we told them was that we would be more than happy to cosign a loan for them in case either one of their credit lines were in bad shape.

That was the worst two weeks of my life. I learned many lessons over that stretch of time. Bob and I got slaughtered. I even accused— no, I knew—Bob H.'s partner was a ringer, a professional dice thrower. I didn't know two guys could bend so low, like snakes in the grass. And what happened to good old-fashioned sportsmanship? Those guys whom Bob D. and I had defeated in the past had always been treated with respect. The toxic garbage that spewed out of their mouths was terrible; I was embarrassed and humiliated that the others watching this match should be exposed to such vulgarity. Shameful.

And that stuff about the "Dice Gods": there are no "Dice Gods." There couldn't have been, ever. I don't think there was even a thing called Luck, because we sure didn't have any. One night I picked up the dice and quietly opened the back door and stepped outside and threw those dice as hard and as far as I could. I almost dislocated my shoulder; it's no bullshit that my arm was sore the next day. At least that gave me some satisfaction. I went back inside and on the table were six shiny new dice. Fuck, I couldn't even recognize my darkest hour. But those other guys would show me.

A penny-a-point, a measly penny. People don't stop on the street to pick up anything less than a quarter. (The exception is my wife, who always picks up those "lucky pennies.") Do you know how many pennies are in one hundred and seventy dollars? If I'm not mistaken, it's about 17,000. That's what I owed after two weeks, and Bob owed the same. I will never again underestimate the power of a penny, and today I, too, find myself picking them up off the ground, unless my wife beats me to it.

This story gets me to thinking about a bar here in town that will cash your paycheck. In the window there is a sign that reads, "We'll cash your check, but round off the change to the nearest dime." I take that to mean that they will end up with a few pennies after cashing every check. Now that doesn't seem like much until you consider that they cash checks twenty-four hours a day, seven days a week. And I read that sign twenty years ago.

CHAPTER 6

WATER WORLD

It was a normal night at work—well, at least what we considered normal. We'd all had our quota of medicine, which now included the famous 714 Quaalude. Actually, we had been taking them for a while, but lately it seemed like were taking more.

This particular evening I can remember being bored, looking for trouble. We had a cue to do, so we all got up and stood by our lines. Looking down the rail, I spotted Big Tom standing there swaying. Either he was swaying to the music, or he was about ready to fall down.

It was then that I had the funniest thought: wouldn't it be funny if I took a couple of pieces of Kleenex tissues and went to the drinking fountain and made a dripping wet spit wad of sorts? Then, next time Big Tom was standing by to do a cue, I'd hit him in the back of his big fat head and watch him have a fit, knowing the rest of the guys would think it was pretty goddamn funny, too.

As I grabbed some tissues, I was laughing uncontrollably. If I kept this up, I'd miss my aim for sure. I waited until Tom was getting ready to do a cue, and sneaked up behind him.

I'm not saying Tom was a baby; it's just that he sort of over-reacted to things. I also knew that he wouldn't be able to catch me. Oh, he'd get a hold of me sooner or later, but I'd deal with that then.

So there I was, standing behind Tom, trying to get myself together.

Knowing that there was a good possibility that I'd miss, I'd come prepared with a couple of spares.

Batter up! I took the classic pitcher's stance, perfect windup and release. A miss, just to the left of his head, but that was okay, because the second one was on its way and it looked right on track.

Tom either saw or heard the first shot because he turned his big old head to the left to see what happened. An instant later, there was a loud smacking sound as the second one smashed into the side of his face.

"Fuck, motherfucker's dead." The spit wad had come apart and part of it had wrapped around Tom's face. Covering most of his nose and one eye, it looked like some kind of freakish ritual war mask. In a way, it was.

I was laughing so hard I was paralyzed, stuck to that spot. Tom put the lock up and was on me so fast I couldn't get away. When Tom wanted to pound on a person, he'd grab you in a bear hug and then pinch your nipples. Hard.

And he had me good; I had tears in my eyes it hurt so much. But this wasn't the first time I'd been in that spot. So I did my bear-hug-break hold: I grabbed his nuts. This time it worked, but other times it had no effect. Tom told me one time that he had practiced sucking up his nuts and that from now on, my hold-breaking move would no longer be effective. Damn if he wasn't telling the truth.

Earlier I said something about events happening and that at the time we didn't know that something significant had just taken place. Well, that moment was one of them. Tom, of course, exacted his revenge minutes later with a perfect shot to the back of my neck, a shot so hard I had a big red spot. Then he or I missed, hit someone else, and naturally they joined in by ambushing some innocent bystander, and so on. The spit wad fight went on to last two or three years.

As the months wore on, the spit wads grew larger. That first day I'd made the "wad heard around the world", using four or five tissues wetted and rolled together, with a dry one wrapped around those, to hold it all in place. A year, year and a half later, one spit wad would require a half box of tissues. Soon the rail was going through more tissue boxes in a week than all other departments in the whole hotel except housekeeping. And that, folks, is the absolute truth, because down in the "help's hall" one day, I heard two guys talking about the increase of the tissue order and that it seemed very excessive. This caught my attention because at first I thought these guys might be Security and maybe they were going to set up a secret sting operation to find out where all the tissues were disappearing.

So I followed them when they left and in a few minutes I was standing outside the purchasing department. Hey, these guys could be worse than Security. It was evident that if our wars were going to continue, we were going to have to find some other source of ammunition, or bring it from home, and none of us could afford that.

There are sixty-three lines, or ropes, on the rail, and there were nights when, before going home as the second show came to a close, I would look down the rail and see that every rope was a mess, with pieces of Kleenex tangled all up and down every last line. There was Kleenex on every light fixture, hanging off of every set piece, high and low. The concrete walls would be covered, too. Dion, our boss, was somehow able to ignore it. At times he was a saint, because we destroyed this place night after night. But as long as we did our cues, it was all right.

There was one guy, whose name I don't recall, who was way ahead of his time. He was on to this recycling thing before most people were. This ingenious fellow took one of the towels we had backstage and tied it into a knot, then took it to the drinking fountain and soaked it with water. He now had a new weapon of destruction that was reusable. Genius.

This new device turned out to be devastating. The first poor bastard who was attacked by this thing was literally taken down to his knees. And then it was improved by tying a short piece of tie line to the end opposite the knot, which allowed you to really get it swinging. I'm not lying when I tell you that I've had the wind knocked out of me by those things.

One night I lay in wait for one of the guys to go by me. I thought that earlier he'd taken a cheap shot at me, so I was there to get even.

Craig H. was the guy I was going to get. I was hiding behind a curtain and through a small hole I could see Craig coming. Just as Craig walked around the curtain, I creamed him. The knot took him high on the forehead, and the sound it made was unpleasant to say the least. Craig did go down, and instantly I had a panic attack. Oh my God, I killed him! But he slowly got to his feet, and when he looked up, he had murder in his eyes. If he hit me, well, I truly deserved it, because I'd delivered the all time "cheap shot."

I had backed away from Craig and was leaning against the ropes on the rail when I could see he was getting ready to charge. Watch out, SHE'S REARING TO BUCK! And here he came. Now I said if he punched me that I deserved it, which was true. But I didn't say I'd let him punch me.

At the last moment I squeezed back through the ropes and Craig went flying by. Because of his momentum and the fact that he lunged at me, then grabbed only air, Craig stumbled and fell again. This time I was on him and wrapped him up in a bear hug of my own.

We were both lying on the ground and I said, "Craig, you have every right to be mad and kick my ass. What I did was uncalled for and you have my deepest apology. Still, I'd prefer you didn't hit me, so we'll stay right here until you cool off."

Finally he told me to get the fuck off him, so I did, but I still wasn't sure he wouldn't try something. So I kept a close eye on him the rest of the evening. No need; Craig ignored me for the next couple of months, and I hate nothing more than someone who won't talk to me. It was decided that for the good of the crew, the knotted weapon would hence be banned from the water sports.

Finally it was a free-for-all, with cups of water, those water bottles with the squirt ends, even your common squirt guns—but they were inadequate. Then someone brought over a white ice bucket, which easily held a gallon or more of water. And it didn't end with the second show any more; you weren't out of danger now until you were locked safely in your car.

It was Big Tom who finally brought the water games to an end. He was running around with a cup of water and he'd finally cornered his prey. He let the water fly and it went right past his target and into our television. After the fire was out, we all stood there looking at the smoldering mess that was once an important piece of equipment.

Tom came in the next night with a new TV and some of us chipped in a few dollars, because any one of us could have been the one who had done that.

So the water games came to an end and things settled down for a while.

CHAPTER 7

ANIMAL HOUSE

Throughout the history of the Folies, animals have been employed from time to time, and one of the most famous was Trojan the horse.

The news of Trojan's arrival spread across the stage weeks before he actually arrived. In anticipation of Trojan's many needs, a shiny little corral was erected outside the large double doors of the backstage area. The corral wasn't very large because after Trojan was led out of his horse trailer, he would only stay in the corral long enough to be harnessed, with a short wait before he was led backstage and hooked up to an eighteenth century-styled carriage.

It fell upon Skip, the prop man, to put the harness on this "magnificent" animal. I don't know what we expected, but Trojan was about eleven years old (how many horse years is that?) and was kind of swaybacked, but all right for a horse, I guess.

Anyway, Trojan's owner, Hank, told Skip that the horse was real laid back. Skip would open the gate, slide in, do his business, then step back out and lock the gate. Meanwhile Hank, who went in and out to do his horse maintenance, finally told Skip he could leave the gate open, as Trojan wouldn't go anywhere; just loop his reins over the top rail of the corral after he put the bridle on.

So the next day Skip went out, opened the gate, and as he turned around to get the bridle, Trojan took off like he was running in the Kentucky Derby. And they're off! Skip saw the horse round the corner and disappear. We were busy with the show and I think it was Hank who finally ran Trojan down somewhere on Las Vegas Boulevard, one of the busiest streets in Las Vegas.

Trojan had a will of his own. And as all animal-show related business goes, unexpected things happen. Trojan's job twice a night was to pull a carriage across the stage, a distance of sixty feet or so, then stop when the carriage reached the offstage area.

Five minutes before Trojan's big carriage-pulling part came, he was led in and hooked up. Maybe five minutes is a long time just to stand there, for a horse; maybe that's like thirty horse minutes, I don't know. However, once in a while, Trojan would take off early.

An eighteenth century carriage definitely looks out of place racing across the stage during a 1930's speakeasy set. Once he took off without the driver, the girl in the carriage screaming all the way. No stopping center stage where she should have been helped down and escorted to the Ball. I don't even know how they stopped the damn thing when it got to the other side of the stage.

Sometimes the most unlikely source can provide people with opportunities to do things that they would ordinarily not be able to do. Case in point: if you take an ordinary plastic baggie, plus one and a half or two dried Trojan horse turds, crush the turds, then roll the baggie up, it looks just like a bag of pot.

This was another one of those pranks you couldn't repeat too often, but then, we had plenty of guys from the Union Hall who would come in for a night or two; we could rely on that source as a constant supply of new victims. We'd pick out some young new guy and see which set of deck cues he was on, and then we'd go to work.

At some point we'd plant the bag where he would be sure to see it, but at the same time we'd make sure that everyone else was not too near. Every one of these new guys picked the bag up, but it's what they did with it that was funny.

Most of the time they would see it, stop, look around, then pick it up; a couple of them did what I would have done, kicked it along until they got offstage and then picked it up. One guy took it directly into the Head Carpenter's office and turned it in. Stay away from that guy.

It was very funny to watch someone take the bag out, open it up and take a deep sniff, expecting the sweet pungent odor of weed, only to be rewarded with the sour stench of horseshit. Yes, I too fell for the bag trick. And you know what? It does smell a lot like shit.

Stagehand as a rule are a pretty close-knit group, so it's no secret that the one thing you don't want to do is piss off a stagehand while he's at work. I've seen it happen and it's just not worth it. Maybe Hank never heard this.

I don't remember what he did to piss us off; it could have been that we just didn't like him. In any event, we screwed with the guy big time. No matter how you look at it, two flat horse trailer tires is a pain in the ass. One truck tire flat and one horse trailer tire flat— same thing, pain in the ass. But to come out and find all your tires flat—some might just cry "Uncle." You had to admire Hank in some respects, because he had the ability to maintain asshole-ness despite adversity. He was going to be a hard nut to crack.

So we waited, patient and observant. And it paid off. Hank fell in love, and every night after the second show he'd wait for his new girl to meet him at the trailer; then he'd walk her to the passenger side, opening the door like a true gentleman.

One of the things that pissed us off was the horseshit he'd leave around; so, one night right before the end of the second show, one of the guys went out and grabbed the big square shovel out of the horse trailer and started to pick up some of the horseshit that had been lying around for too long, and put it right through the open window of Hank's truck. And he didn't stop until the show ended.

"Watch this," he said. Hank followed his normal routine, except this time when he opened the door for his girlfriend, buckets of horseshit tumbled out, and I knew he wanted someone, anyone, punished. Someone would pay.

This was one of the few times that the Entertainment Director, our boss, stepped in and asked us to give the guy some slack, otherwise he'd have to get involved and he really didn't want t do that. You know the saying, "the shit started to fly"? Well, the shit stopped flying. As wild and whacked-out as we were, we knew who our boss was, and he was too good to us to fuck over.

One of the pet peeves that Larry, our boss, had was Stagehand parking behind the backstage area. Of course like all good Stagehand it was our job to challenge his authority. When Trojan was brought into the show it cut down on some of the parking area out back.

Jack Y., a flyman on the rail for many years, was the proud owner of a brand-new Cadillac, lime green with all the extras. It was a beautiful two-door De Ville, just off the lot.

Because we arrived at work before Hank did, sometimes the parking got a little screwed up, especially if Stagehand were parked out back. And perhaps because he had his new car, Jack figured that parking out back would be safer, to preserve that new car finish for as long as possible. A sensible train of thought.

Things seldom work out like we plan, and so it was the same with Jack. Hank, who would arrive thirty minutes after the show started, could not always find easy parking, especially since he was towing a horse trailer. So one night Hank was forced to back his trailer near the corral, which caused the rear end of the trailer to stop not too far from Jack's new car.

As the men would unhook Trojan from his carriage, they would walk him across the upstage area and lead him out the back door, turning him over to Hank. Hank would lead Trojan over to the back of the trailer and tie him up to the back ramp.

How do I put this delicately? Trojan had pulled his last carriage, worn his last bridle; he'd never need another horseshoe. You get the picture: tied to the back of the trailer, Trojan suffered a heart attack. Evidently, Trojan had enough line to enable him to walk close to Jack's new car, and that was where he suffered his attack. When Trojan fell, he shook with great spasms; this, for Jack's new car, was very unfortunate. Every spasm that rocked Trojan's body resulted in his hoofs crashing into the driver's side of Jack's car. By the time the poor horse was finally silent, Jack's car was destroyed. Jack had walked outside but came right back in; he couldn't stand to watch. We could, though, and we told Jack, "See what happens when you don't follow the parking rules?" He told us to "Get fucked."

We had monkeys, too: Gene and his chimp act. They were pretty good, but everyone learned quickly that the chimps were not ones to fuck with.

Gene had a truck with a huge camper shell on the back, and this was home to the chimps while they were on the road. Since they parked directly behind the backstage area, there were many nights we could hear them from inside. Outside, there would be a terrible racket. Until Gene went in, you'd hear some loud yelling, a couple of bangs, and then all would be quiet.

When the chimps were brought on stage, everyone gave them plenty of room. These were incredibly strong animals. One night during one of the shows, a drunken woman rushed up on stage to touch or pet one of the cute little chimps. If I'm not mistaken it was the baby chimp, which did look very cute, all dressed up in baby clothes. When the lady got close, the baby chimp reached out and grabbed her ankle and flipped her up in the air. She escaped the ordeal relatively intact, but those of us backstage who saw it happen had a newfound respect for these animals.

Now I have never claimed to be the smartest guy in the world, and it's a good thing that I never did, because there is ample evidence to the contrary. So it comes as no surprise that I had to learn for myself.

When Gene was on stage, I could peek through the downstage masking and there, sitting on these little chairs, were the chimps. For the most part they were well behaved and quiet. It was always the baby that would start the shit flying, sometimes literally. If Gene didn't quiet things down quickly, the other two chimps would also start acting up. Gene had a short wooden dowel about three and a half feet long, and used it to discipline the chimps. Usually a short, light crack to their backsides would do the trick.

These chimps were so human-like in so many ways it was incredible; when they performed well and were rewarded, I'd swear to Christ they'd smile. When they were punished, they'd pout.

One night I was peeking out the curtain looking at the chimps when the little chimp started to act up. Gene promptly dealt with him and walked back on stage. I was laughing and stuck my head through the curtain and made a face at the little guy, then said something like,

"Ha, ha, you got in trouble," and even pointed my finger at him. I pulled my head back through the curtain. All of a sudden something hit me hard in the thigh. Son of a bitch, that hurt. A couple of inches over and it would have been right in the nuts. I looked back through the curtain in time to see the little chimp sit back down in his chair.

Shit, that little bastard just slugged me in the leg. I went limping off to do my cues. Later, during one of the acts, I went to the restroom, took my pants down, and saw a bruise the size of a grapefruit on my thigh. Thank God it wasn't one of the bigger chimps.

This convinced me that these animals are smarter than I gave them credit for being. I decided to leave them alone. Now who's the smarter one? Never mind.

Besides some birds and a couple of dogs, we were animal-free in the Folies show for years to come.

CHAPTER 8

BROKEN BONES AND BLOOD

Time ticked on and we did our jobs, tested our drugs, and always looked for new trouble to get into. Once again we prevailed.

One night Bob D., my best friend, found me right after we'd made our pre-sets, and took me aside in a very mysterious manner. I was thinking, "Bob's got some weed, maybe some mushrooms or something."

Bob unzipped his coat and cautiously pulled out a large Zip-Loc baggie. Oh boy! This has got to be some good shit! Maybe something new I hadn't had before. Opening the bag carefully, he held it up for me to inspect. Peyote, maybe? No, but surely some natural plant-type psychedelic I was eager to ingest.

I reached in and…"Shit!" That hurt. What the hell was in this bag?

Bob said, "Cockle burrs," with a smile, the joke going completely over my head. These burrs were round, about the size of my thumb, and completely covered with needle-sharp thorns.

"Cockle burrs," I said. "What the fuck are we supposed to do with cockle burrs? Do they get you high?"

"No, stupid, but wait and see."

Well, the show started, and after a while Bob grabbed me again and said, "Follow me." I followed Bob until we were standing in the dark ten feet off the rail.

"So?" I said.

"Quiet."

A few seconds later, here came Big Tom walking down the rail to do a cue.

Like I said before, Big Tom was usually the person who seemed to be chosen to endure a new prank or have a joke played on him. His reactions were so goddamn funny that you never knew what to expect. And Tom, bless his heart, never stayed angry for long—but he did get even.

So there we were, Bob and I, watching Tom get ready to work. He pulled the rope out and with both arms raised above his head, stood waiting for the right music cue. Then he would pull down hard on the rope and complete his cue. When his arms were over his head, out of the corner of my eye, I saw a quick movement.

A moment later I saw two or three small yellow dots appear on Tom's back, and an instant later heard him say, "Oh fuck, what the fuck's on my back?" He was kind of dancing around, one hand on the rope, the other reaching around to his back, frantically trying to locate what was biting him or whatever the hell was happening.

Of course, now Tom had to do his cue; using extreme willpower and a lot of crying, Tom pulled his rope. I almost felt sorry for him. Okay, so I didn't; watching that big guy was pretty funny. When he was done with his cue, he tried to walk so that these burrs caused the least amount of pain while he moved.

I ran over to Tom with a semi-straight face, the best I could manage, and said, "Hey, big guy, wait a minute. What's wrong?"

"Get away," Tom said. "Just get the fuck away. I know you had something to do with this, and paybacks are a mother fucker." Of that I had no doubt.

But I had already plucked one of these things off his back, which extracted a small whimpering sound from Tom, and it was nasty looking. I held it up for Tom to see, and said, "Gee, that's pretty weird looking; where in the hell did that come from?"

"Oh yeah, I wonder where that came from?" Tom answered. "I just wonder."

Way to go, Bob. Who knows where this is going to lead? I now realized that there could be hundreds of burrs in the large bag that

Bob had shown me. Not only that, but I recalled Bob saying something about having more at home.

The war was on, but unlike the water wars, where all you did was go find a box of Kleenex, Bob didn't just hand a bunch of these burrs out. Oh no, the only way to get these babies was to pick them off another person, find one on the floor, or (unfortunately, the most common way) pull them off your own body.

"Christ, these things hurt," was the first thought that went through my mind as I was hit about the neck and shoulders. Maybe Tom wasn't such a baby. I kind of felt like crying myself. Once again, nowhere to hide, and no one could be trusted.

I don't know how many times I would be called over by someone for a seemingly innocent conversation, only to walk away and be stabbed in the back. It wasn't uncommon to be hit thirty, maybe forty times a night in the back or chest. And the worst, the very worst place, was to take a hit on the nipple. God, that hurt!

One night I took a magnifying glass and performed a closer inspection of these burrs, and found that on the tip of each needle was a little barb, much like a fishing hook. No wonder these damn things stuck so well. Every once in a while you'd do more damage to yourself by picking up and throwing these things at your target than he could do by firing at you.

I can recall coming home one night and in the bedroom, when I took my shirt off, hearing my wife gasp, "Phil, my God, what happened to you?" By that time I'd forgotten about work, so I didn't know what she was talking about.

I think that when I say I really hated those things, I speak for everyone. Sometimes when I'd leave after the second show, I couldn't even lean back against the car seat. What was most irritating was that when someone snatched a burr off your back, the little needles didn't always come out. If you've ever had a splinter, then you know what a pain in the ass it can be.

The test for manhood happens in many different ways. In some cultures it's a ritual, a planned event. For the rest of us life provides the test. Little did we know that this was Big Tom's day, his passage into manhood.

As usual, we were all getting in our cheap shots. Tom, who was my favorite target, was just engaging the lock after doing a cue and was starting to walk up-rail. After carefully reviewing the incident afterwards, I concluded that my timing was a little off. I do remember really winding up. I really wanted this shot to count and gave it extra effort. However, as soon as that cockle burr left my hand, I knew it was off the mark. Too high and slicing to the left. Tom's as big as a barn, which proves that I'm not the best shot in the world, especially when I'm excited.

"Fuck me," I said, and for Tom that translated into, "Oh my God, I'm hit. Medic, Christ, someone call 911."

Panic flooded my body. Tom was holding his head, little sobbing sounds escaping through his cupped hands. My God, I thought, I've hit him in the eye. How could this have happened? Then Tom was kneeling on one leg. Oh God, he's going to die and I'll be up on murder charges, lose my job, family, the whole bit. All because of a cockle burr.

I ran up to Tom and yelled, "Where did I hit you? Where did I hit you?" Tom was mumbling something, his hands covering his face. I thought, that's why I can't hear him.

Grabbing his hands, I said, "Tom, you gotta put your hands down. I need to see what's wrong." I was in a state of full-blown panic. I knew I was going to see lots of blood, and I knew from experience that eye injuries are always nasty.

Finally Tom lowered his hands and I prepared for the worst. None of us had ever meant to hurt anyone. All that was going through my mind was that old saying I used to hear as a kid: "It's all fun and games until somebody puts an eye out."

His eyes were okay. Sweet Jesus, his eyes were okay! Relief from a stressful situation is one of the greatest feelings on this earth.

Then I started to laugh. There on Tom's lower lip, stuck like a stick in the mud, was the cockle burr. His lip was just starting to swell a little, which gave him a pouty look. Tom would pull on it a little, then moan when he'd have to let go; it just hurt too much to pull it out.

"Tom," I said, "Hold still; I'll have it off of you in a second." I reached for the cockle burr.

"No, no, no, wait, don't do anything. It's too sore to touch!" He held his hand over his lip.

Now we were dealing with a medical situation here; now we were playing in my backyard. I hate to say it, but I've dealt with three-year-olds whose skinned knees were worse injuries than Tom's, and who displayed a higher tolerance for pain. What we needed here was a distraction. Just for a second, I needed Tom to take his big paw away from his face. "If you're a big boy and put your hands down, I'll give you a sucker." You know your trouble, Tom? You don't have a sense of humor.

We stood there for a minute or two, and by now most of the rail crew had passed by; little fits of laughter and snickering couldn't help but be heard. Now Tom was starting to get pissed.

I said, "Tom, let's go over to the mirror and take a better look; then we'll take it out."

"Okay," he muttered, and I started to turn like I was going to walk away. Out of the corner of my eye I saw Tom's hands come down. I turned back real fast, and before he could react, I grabbed that cockle burr and pulled—well, actually, more like tore—it from his lip.

"Oh, Jesus, what the fu…hey, you got it out." He realized what I'd done. Thank God he hadn't seen the small, spurting spray of blood that shot out for a moment. He probably would have fainted.

In the end, Tom and I entered into a treaty, a lot like the U.S. and Japan did after we dropped the atomic bomb. I had his unconditional surrender, and in return my attacks would cease immediately. Later, when some new form of conflict was discovered, I had to explain to Tom that he hadn't read the fine print: our treaty only referred to "Cockle Burr Warfare."

One year the guys on the rail received the ultimate gift—for a child, which explains why we were so excited. A trampoline, and a big one at that. Actually, as you've probably guessed already, no one in their right mind would give six stoned-to-the-bone rail guys a toy like this just to amuse themselves. But someone did decide that a flying trapeze act would be nice to have during the show, and so one day we came to work and found this great big toy that obviously none of us had possessed as a kid.

As I've said before, this was a huge trampoline. It was a miracle that we could even set it up in the space we had, because by nature the area backstage is a pretty packed place. However, in order for the act to take place, it had to "live" somewhere (to "live" means to have a spot where a prop or piece of scenery stays during a show). It ended up stage left, down toward the front of—you guessed it—the rail.

Of course, we believed we were all seasoned professionals, even though only a couple of us had ever set foot on a trampoline. It must have been pretty funny to see five grown fucked-up men jumping up and down on a trampoline. One thing we learned quickly was that five people were too many.

The trampoline was placed in a cramped space with a concrete wall immediately to the left; on the right, right where the shadow box use to be, was a two-story motorized tower. The tower was designed to look like part of a 1930's Chicago apartment building. On the backside of the tower was a staircase leading to the second story, and at the top of this staircase was a door opening onto a balcony. To be precise, the door was actually a large window. You could step through this window onto the balcony. The balcony measured two feet wide, and it wrapped around three quarters of the tower. So a portion of the balcony faced the trampoline.

For a couple of days we all took turns bouncing, but you know what? That got boring real fast. Now I remember the one bad thing about trampolines, and it's the fact that you can only do so much on them.

After doing a cue one night I had to check something on stage, so I walked down by the trampoline area. You know the feeling you get when you're aware that something is happening, but you just can't tune into it for one reason or another? I felt, more than saw, something pass over my head. A second later Rob P. landed on the trampoline, bounced way up in the air, and smacked into the concrete wall. Then he slid down the wall and fell back onto the trampoline.

"Whew! That was a rush." Rob was already moving to edge off the trampoline and was ready for more action.

"Christ, Rob, where did you come from?" I asked.

Rob was already at the corner of tower and said, "Follow me." Up the stairs we went, and out onto the balcony. Following along the balcony, we turned the corner and stopped.

As I looked over the edge I understood what had just happened. That little feeling I'd had earlier was right on the money. Rob had climbed up on the railing and had jumped off the tower, flown over ten feet of concrete floor, and landed on the trampoline. That crazy son of a bitch.

When the trampoline was set up, its canvas surface was approximately three and a half feet off the ground. The tower balcony was eighteen feet high. That makes the drop from the balcony to the trampoline about fifteen and a half feet. No, that's wrong, because Rob stood on top of the railing, so another three and a half feet should be added. Nineteen feet total. That's a pretty fair drop.

This was a classic example of what an idle mind can do. Before I could say another word, Rob leaped from the rail again. For an instant I had a terrible image of a person leaping to his death, the classic suicide attempt. Rob's rebound off the trampoline took him almost as high as the balcony. Now, Rob's been mentioned earlier, and it would be an erroneous idea to consider him as retarded or slightly dimwitted. I believe it's the exact opposite; Rob is a very intelligent person but he's a thrill seeker and his sense of humor shouldn't be, in fact couldn't be, judged by normal standards. That pretty much applied to all of us railbirds, and is probably why we all got along so well for so many years.

The first time I jumped off the tower it was quite a thrill. It was also farther than it looked. "Remember, you have to push off hard so you don't fall short of the trampoline." That was damn good advice from Rob, but that was a given. The old adrenalin was pumping as I pushed off the rail. I wanted to let out an Indian war cry but I didn't, in case I missed. It was a gas; even though I have never liked the sensation of falling, this was pretty neat.

Right before you'd hit the trampoline, you would try to make sure no body parts were in weird positions or unprotected. And you did hit pretty hard. I chose to land on my butt that first time, because I feared if I landed on my feet my ankles would snap, then one or both legs would break, or a leg bone would dislocate and get shoved right up my ass, and as that is still virgin territory, well, we wouldn't want that.

I guess I just didn't have the guts to get too crazy; truth was, in the rational part of my thinking (in the times when I could think rationally), I knew what we were doing was very dangerous.

For reasons that I'll explain later, I found that I did many things because everyone else on the rail was doing them, just like kids do, and I do regret a part of that. It wasn't until years later that I finally started to mature. I'll tell you now that the major reason was the use of the drugs and the alcohol. But no matter what, all things considered, most things were a hell of a lot of fun.

In some aspects, Big Tom and I were a lot alike; neither one of us, when we got mad, could stay angry very long and didn't like confrontations. I know that during the few times Tom was genuinely upset at me, or yelled at me, it wouldn't be more than a couple of minutes until he would walk over and apologize, even if he was right. Also, like me, Tom did things he didn't really want to do but he went along with them. And even though he never came right out and told me so, jumping off the tower was one of those things he really didn't want to do.

Tom had five or six successful jumps under his belt, certainly not amateur status in our eyes. I noticed one time as I stood behind him waiting my turn that as Tom, who if you'll remember was six-four or six-five and two hundred and fifty pounds, stood on the balcony rail, it would bend out a little and make those sounds that things make when there's too much pressure on them. Obviously the railing was built as a decorative piece, never intended for bearing that amount of weight.

One night Tom was preparing for another leap. I was watching him from down below; Rob and a couple of other guys joined me. As Tom stepped up on the railing we could hear the creaking noises. As soon as Tom put his full weight on the railing, the bolts securing the rail to the balcony floor started pulling right through the plywood. For one of the few times ever, we stopped laughing.

You will hear people talk about an event or an accident and sometimes they'll recall things happening in slow motion, and that's exactly how I remember this.

The railing slowly bent outwards. Tom started to grab at anything he could hang onto, but there was nothing. At the last moment, when it seemed the railing was going to fall off, Tom managed to push off, hoping to go out far enough so he would hit the trampoline and not the concrete floor.

Seeing the big guy fall, screaming like a mad man falling to his death—and for all he knew, he was—those big arms flapping so fast and wildly, I thought maybe, just maybe they'll act like wings, oh stop it, there is no goddamn way in hell that this guy will do anything remotely related to flying, in fact, he's plunging down faster than a ton of bricks.

"Please don't die," were the words on my lips. "He's gonna make it, sweet Jesus, he's gonna make it."

Well, he sort of made it. One leg touched the canvas; the other missed and went through the area between the canvas and the frame, where the springs are. In that sense he was very lucky, lucky to be living. When Tom's leg scraped down the side of the canvas, he got a skin peel. But what he said really hurt was his nuts.

Tom just stayed there for a minute, silent as a mute. Then he looked up and said, "That hurt." The way he said it was really funny, very monotone. He told us he was all right and didn't need any help. We all started to walk away, but I looked back.

Tom took a minute to untangle himself, trying not to aggravate his injuries. He looked like a puppet—all these weird jerky movements. Finally he was free, and he slowly limped off into the sunset. I had to give him credit; I know it hurt like hell and he never complained. He didn't whimper once.

Little did we know that perhaps this incident was a preview for the upcoming attraction, in which Tom would be the star.

The trapeze act provided other items that snared us, snared our imaginations, just like moths drawn to a light: huge, thick mats.

Because of the height restrictions of the stage, the performers weren't terribly high off the deck, not like you'd see at a circus. So instead of a safety net, four big blue folding mats were put down on the ground. Unfolded, each one was about eight feet wide and ten feet long. Put them all together and you had a giant mat sixteen feet wide and twenty feet long.

One of the set pieces in the show at that time was a large rolling deck. There was also a second deck the same height as the first but not as wide. On stage, during the set they were used in, they were pinned together to make one large deck. I can't for the life of me remember how it was used, or what took place on top of it. But none of that mattered. What was important is the fact that one of the guys realized, when the mats were laid out, they were slightly larger than the deck.

One thing about Stagehands is that they never forget where a comfortable place to lie down and take a nap is located. And if there aren't any good places around, they will create one. So, while all the rest of us failed to grasp the opportunity, one person did not.

After we were told about this new idea, we knew it was a good one. With a few small hurdles to clear, we'd have a nice place to lie down and take a short nap, which all daycare centers will tell you is essential for kids so they won't get cranky. It's important for kids to play nice when they're together.

Anyway, we finally convinced the prop department that it would be to their advantage if they left the mats unfolded on the rolling decks. That way, instead of carrying them, they could roll them all downstage at once, then unload them. The mats were used right before the deck, so it worked out great because when the deck was being struck (taken offstage), they could stop real fast, load the mats back on the rolling decks, and just roll everything back upstage all at once, nice and tidy.

Now that we had explained to the prop guys that we were just watching out for their best interests, and it did seem to make quite a bit of sense, we convinced them to try it out during the second show; you know, get the feel of it and start saving themselves a lot of work.

Whatever rumors you might hear about Stagehands, being stupid probably won't be one of them. Sure, we do dumb things from time to time, but who doesn't? Just in case you have any doubts, check out a show sometime, but do it from backstage if possible. Watch even a small show—the technology, the lighting, sound, pyro (fireworks), construction, rigging—I've been doing this for twenty-seven years and have met some remarkable and truly talented people.

So it only makes sense that the Head Prop man said, "That's a good idea guys, and I'm deeply touched that you guys on the rail would be so concerned for the welfare of us prop guys, but what bothers me is, I know you guys. So would it be too much trouble for you all to stop the bullshit and tell me what's really going on?"

Wow, that hurt; man, you really know how to hurt a guy. See what happens when you try to look out for your fellow union brothers? Here we are trying to make your job as easy as possible and you have the nerve to accuse us of having ulterior motives. How dare you?

"Cut the bullshit or the mats stay where they are and I don't care if it is easier. So what will it be?"

He's tough, no doubt about it. It turns out the guy was a veteran stagehand with well over twenty years in the business. There wasn't much he hadn't seen or done. Oh! And yes, he had his own private little sleeping nook underneath the stage right Can-Can set. It was understood in no uncertain terms that trespassers would be prosecuted to the full extent of the law; in other words, that was his spot, and his alone.

Best to come clean in this situation. "Okay, we need a place to crash, and if you decide to go along with our idea, we'll even load and unload the mats for you guys. So do we have a deal?"

"You boys drive a hard bargain, but okay, we got a deal." Because we were so loaded and because he was such a shrewd negotiator, we really screwed ourselves. In fact, that's sugar coating the word "fuck." It wasn't until six or seven months later that we found out just what a "deal" he'd actually given us, and if he were alive today he'd still chuckle.

We were in heaven, on easy street; now, after we wore ourselves out doing "whatever", we had a nice soft mat to lie down on and rest a little. Sometimes all of us could be found lounging around on the mats. We tried to make sure one guy always stayed awake, but it was only a matter of time before our sentry would also fall asleep, leaving us in a very bad position. But that wouldn't happen for months to come.

We worked as a team when it came time for us to load and unload those mats. Two guys to a mat, a total of four guys making two trips, then the same thing when it came time to load them back up. No doubt about it, we really got a good deal; shit, we were ready to join the U.N., show all those dumb sons of bitches just how the bargaining process works. It was a goddamn shame our talents were being wasted away in that dump.

Only one thing kind of bothered me. (I should have called the prop man by his name so as not to confuse you: the name was Stan C.) Sometimes when I'd walk by the Can-Can set, I'd see Stan in his little bungalow and kid with him. I'd tell him it was too bad that his place was in the low rent district, under the set and all. I referred to our mats as the luxury high rise because, unlike his spot, which you almost had to get on your hands and knees to get into, our mats were up off the ground and we even had a staircase to walk up, if you were too lazy to jump. I told him if he wanted to see what the luxury high rise was like, he'd have to come over to our side. However, at the moment we had no vacancies, but perhaps we could put him on the waiting list. And if something did become available we would certainly consider him.

Old Stan would just laugh—laugh until he had tears in his eyes, then tell me something to the effect that real estate was a good investment. Like our so-called luxury condos—they might be the hottest thing going one day, and the next day we might be lucky to have a bed to sleep in. What was that all about? Was Stan getting senile? Fuck, if you couldn't just joke with him without getting some whacked-out speech in return, then I just wouldn't talk to him.

It turned out that old Stan just couldn't hold in the joke any longer. By now we had been using the mats for months. For all intents and purposes it was our special place, for the rail guys only.

Stan came over to the mat condos one night and said, "Hi, guys. As the head prop man, and the person whom you guys dealt with in regard to these mats, well, I guess I'm the one who should break the bad news to you."

"Bad news? What bad news? Oh, the news that refers to your tooth? The last real one fell out or something?" Yeah, that was funny, we were all laughing, it was so stupid. (That reminds me of a little joke that I'll tell you in a moment.)

"Nope," he said. "The news is…how should I put it? In a month or so, your lease is up. Consider this to be your eviction notice."

What the fuck was he talking about? "Okay, as you would put it, Stan, stop the bullshit and spit it out."

"Well, in a little over a month from now, those big rolling deck pieces are going out the door, out of the show. They're going to be replaced by six brass beds in a new number that's coming into the show."

We were shocked; this was bad news, the worst possible news ever. It couldn't get any worse than this, could it?

"Oh yeah, there's one other thing. After we all made that little deal, the one where you guys load and unload the mats—well, since then, my prop crew have other cues now, so I talked it over with the head carpenter and he decided it's best if you guys continue to handle the mats. So when the time comes, you'll have to get them out from where we used to store them, preset them for us, and when they come back offstage, you'll store them again. Now before you decide to kill the messenger, you should know that your boss, Dion, agrees with us and said that it sounds good to him. Have a good day. 'Bye."

"Wait a minute!" someone yelled. "We've been watching you make these beds for a while now, working on them every so often. So tell me, how long have you known about this?"

"To tell you the truth, it's been in the plans for about eight months or so." Stan answered. So that was what that bastard meant when he was talking about real estate and "the next day not having a bed to sleep in." He wasn't kidding, because these "beds" just had a sheet stretched over the top with nothing underneath, so you couldn't lie down on them. A used car salesman had nothing on this guy. There went our U.N. dreams.

Before I forget, here's that little joke I promised: What's the number one pick-up line a guy says to a girl in Arkansas? "Nice tooth." Ha, ha.

During the months in which we did have access to the mats, Rob suggested to us that perhaps we weren't using the mats to their greatest potential. It was how he suggested this new idea that was unique.

We were lying on the mats relaxing when Rob came bouncing upstairs. Tom was in the center lying on his back, and complained to Rob that he was shaking the deck too much. What actually came out was more like, "Hey, lie down, be still, and shut the fuck up, you queer."

Rob, never one to shy away from a challenge, spoken or unspoken, jumped up in the air and yelled, "Hey, Tom, it's big time wrestling!" If Rob hadn't done some wrestling in high school or at some time in his life, I'd be surprised. He landed across Tom's stomach, grabbed one knee and pulled it toward him, with his other arm locked around Tom's neck. Tom was officially "pinned."

"Hey, what the fuck are you doing, you fag? Get off me," Tom said. "What are you, crazy? Let go of me."

But Rob really had him pinned. While he continued to hold Tom down, he explained the rules to Tom. "Now Tom, that kind of talk won't get you anywhere. If you want to get up—I mean, give up—you need to slap the mat three or four times. That means you quit."

"Get off, queer."

"Slap the mat."

"Will you get off me before I slap the shit out of you?"

"No, slap the mat, fat boy."

"Rob, get the fuck off me, I'm not kidding."

"Slap the mat."

We were all very impressed; that little fucker really had Tom pinned, because Tom had tried a couple of moves to try and flip Rob off, but they hadn't worked. Now Tom was starting to breathe in a ragged manner and his body had broken out in a sweat.

By now the time was approaching for us to get up and head back to the rail to do our next cue.

"Rob, I gotta get up to do my cue; let me the fuck up."

"Slap the mat."

I was up and heading back to the rail when I heard faint little slapping noises behind me.

"Louder. Really slap the mat."

"Christ."

Now I was almost to the rail and I heard it: loud slaps.

Tom came running over to his place just in time. He was pissed, sweating like a pig, and you could almost believe he'd just finished running a five thousand meter race, except that one look at him would tell you that a hundred yard race between him and a desert tortoise might require a photo finish.

Tom promised all sorts of inhumane acts of retribution to be administered to Rob's body; quite impressive really, though more than a few were anatomically impossible. Good God, what an imagination that man had. If Tom could do a portion of what he was suggesting, Rob would look like some weird human experiment performed by a psychopathic sex-offending surgeon.

WWF wrestling had begun. The mats, which had formerly been a place of refuge, now became an arena of chaos. Once again, set pieces nearby became launching pads for human rockets who feared nothing.

If a guy tried to sneak over to the mat area hoping to enjoy a few minutes of rest and relaxation, he soon found himself buried under a mountain of flesh. One time after a brutal avalanche of bodies untangled and rolled off the poor bastard on the bottom, I took a quick count of the pounds that had been on top of him. Four guys piled up: 250 lbs., 210 lbs., 185 lbs., and 195 lbs. That's 840 pounds on top of the guy, plus a couple of guys who leaped down on the dummy from 15 feet up or so. Once the man was pinned, the other guys just ran over and piled on.

Bloody noses, cut lips, occasional black eyes and the use of Ace bandages and ice were not uncommon. Nor did anyone complain when they'd have to retire for a week or so, due to bruised ribs or twisted body parts. It was the classic battle; perhaps it was the battle of the reincarnation of David and Goliath. This contest had deep roots. The combatants, seasoned veterans, were familiar with the other's tactics as a result of countless encounters on the mats.

If you haven't guessed by now, I'm referring to the two people involved in that very first wrestling bout. I use the word "bout" because the word "match", as in wrestling match, would indicate two individuals evenly matched in the art of wresting. As described earlier, this was not the case.

Yes, Big Tom and Rob were facing off. Rob, the smaller person, outweighed by at least sixty to eighty pounds, also had to deal with a height disadvantage of four to five inches. But Rob was quick and strong and certainly possessed the endurance and tenacity required to compete with a guy Tom's size.

Tom, on the other hand, was, well, big; I think he believed that for him personally, the simpler the better, so he took his best wrestling move and practiced and practiced it until he could execute it in his sleep. Here's what he did: Tom would corner his opponent and grab any body part within reach. Once Tom got a hold of you he would position himself so he could deliver the final blow. It was the devastating "I'll fall on you with all my weight" move. Simple grab and crush. As a little added bonus, once he had you down and was crushing the holy life out of your body, he'd pinch-twist your nipples. He did it so hard to me one time I swore he'd pulled them off.

For sure, this had all the makings of a championship bout. There we were, watching these two titans of the mats and we couldn't even place a wager, because that would have been illegal. Anyway, the air was charged with electricity.

It was shameful. If I hadn't known any better I'd say it was fixed, except for one little reason. They had faced off, circling each other, and Tom lunged for Rob. Knowing of Tom's only tactic, Rob countered the move by stepping to one side. Tom's huge body created its own momentum like a large forest fire creating its own wind currents.

Rob had made one mistake; he didn't get far enough away, and as Tom's body went flying by, Rob was also sucked in. The two went tumbling out of control over the edge of the mats, into the dark abyss. In truth, they only fell about four feet onto the concrete floor, but Rob landed on one of Tom's ankles.

"My God, my ankle's broken!" Tom screamed. "God, oh God, my ankle!" By now we were standing around the two men. Rob was running his hand over a huge knot on his forehead; he might even have been out for a couple of seconds, judging by the expression on his face.

Tom was trying to get untangled, and every time his ankle touched anything he'd scream out in pain. It took all of us to get him up off the floor and into a chair by the rail. Tom finally reached down, forced his shoe off, and pulled his pant leg up to view his injured ankle. He almost passed out.

Giant Polish sausage, was the first thought that came into my mind. For sure it was ugly, all purplish-brown and already quite swollen. Very ugly. Someone came back with a towel packed with ice and laid it gently over the ankle, which caused tears to form in Tom's eyes. We covered his cues for the remainder of the show. Then a couple of us helped Tom out to his car, although he insisted on walking under his own power most of the way.

It was a long time ago, so I'm not sure if he broke it or suffered a severe sprain, but Tom had to take some time off of work, and when he returned he was wearing a cast for quite a while. I seem to remember something about a severe sprain being as bad or worse than some breaks, but I'm not sure it was in reference to Tom's case.

Epilogue: Tom's career as a big-time wrestler had come to a startling end. He was cut down in the prime of his career and resumed working as a union stagehand. This lack of activity caused him to gain weight. At 300 pounds, he would tell you everything was fine until that accident.

Rob went on to be crowned champion of the wrestling circuit at the Tropicana Hotel. Now he held two titles: Wrestling Champion and Undisputed Fart King. What's left for a man after achieving such praise and admiration from his peers? He was elevated to a status he alone possessed. Perhaps that was his downfall. Maybe that's why, less than a year later, he was playing with cockroaches and drawing pornographic "Phantom Peters" all throughout the backstage area.

We'll get into that later on.

Skip R., a very dedicated and knowledgeable stagehand, had an unusual accident one day. For some reason I wasn't there that day, but heard about it from some reliable sources.

The day of the accident was just like any normal day and Skip was especially excited because of the carpentry work involved. As a prop man and carpenter, it was his responsibility to maintain existing props and also to design and build new ones to be used in the show.

In an area near two big double doors backstage we set up our table saw, metal cutoff saw, drill press, welders, and other machinery. Against a portion of one wall, Skip had a small supply of lumber. This included six or seven sheets of 4 foot by 8 foot, three quarter inch thick plywood; some masonite; and a few other assorted pieces of material.

If you've ever worked in a woodshop or scenery shop, you may have experienced a situation in which you needed, let's say, plywood, and what you need is buried all the way in the back. I've experienced it many times and it's a minor pain in the ass. If you're working alone it's a real headache to move the stack of wood, then restack it after you've pulled out the piece you want.

So if my sources are correct, that was the case on this fateful day. Skip and a couple of other guys were working on a project and needed to move part of the wood stack to get to the materials they needed. Sheets of 4x8 three-quarter plywood were given to Skip, who would temporarily hold them up by standing behind them while the other men tried to reach what they needed.

Skip now had three or four sheets leaning against him, when something happened and he was overpowered by the weight. I don't recall the exact explanation of how Skip ended up in the position of being pinned by sheets of plywood, but when he got clear of the pile of wood, he informed his partners that he was bleeding. One of them told Skip that he was missing part of his ear.

In the end, Skip and his ear parts made a hasty trip to the emergency room, where a dedicated team of nurses and doctors did their best to put him back together. I soon began to call him Skipear, pronounced "skip-ear"—get it? Well, okay, that was about the same response I got the first time I saw Skip talking with a few other crew members and I stepped up and told Skip I had a new nickname for him. Nobody laughed. What's wrong guys, it's kinda funny, isn't it? ...Okay, I'll just be over on the rail if you need me. Nobody came.

I generally liked Skip and I respected his work ethics on stage. Skip was a talented person and I believe that he was passed over for Department Head several times, a position he was qualified for and deserving of. The reasons aren't important but I thought he handled it better than I ever could. I admired his determination to hold his head up high and do his work without complaint. Very admirable, in my opinion.

Skip also had a hell of a sense of humor, but it might be described as "dry." There were quite a few times that I'd get home and laugh at something I'd recall Skip saying earlier that night.

However, as far as practical jokes go, I really got Skip good, and even though he swore that he'd get even with me, he never did.

During our world famous Can-Can number, many props were used. It was a set that looked like a type of dance hall in Paris around the late 1800's. Two huge set pieces with stair units sat on stage left and stage right, with about twelve feet separating them at center stage. In front of the stage left set was a long bar unit, and downstage in front of both sets, the prop guy set up round tables with chairs around them. Little plastic drinking glasses sat on the tables.

This Can-Can number used to be the finale, or last number in our show, before the main curtain was lowered. The number lasted about seven minutes. In the last minute or so of the number, two dancers, one carrying a table, the other a chair, would carry them over to the left side of the stage and set them down behind the number one leg.

Our stage uses five pairs of curtains called legs, one leg for each side of the stage. The first set, or number one leg, is almost all the way down stage. By the way, these legs are only about eight feet wide, but twenty-odd feet high. The purpose of a leg is to prevent the audience from looking into the offstage area during the show. The legs also can mask from view people, props or set pieces waiting to go on stage.

The number one leg is only twenty feet or so from the audience. Skip waited there every night for the table and chair carried by the two dancers; as soon as the main curtain was in, he'd set the chair on the table and push both over to the stage left Can-Can set piece. He'd put the chair on the bar unit, then load the table on a little deck built into the backside of the set piece.

Being the observant person that I am, I noticed that as soon as the dancers set the pieces down, Skip would sit down on the chair and put his feet up on the table; then he'd tip back until only the back two chair legs were on the ground. Now he was relaxed and very comfortable waiting for the main curtain to come in, and the end of the show.

For six months I thought about how funny it would be to take out or fly out that curtain "leg" as soon as Skip had relaxed in his chair, feet up, in his kicked back mode. With the leg suddenly out Skip would be sitting there, twenty feet from nine hundred audience members, looking just a little out of place in his blacks (all-black stagehand clothing).

I realized later that because of the amount of action going on all around the stage, perhaps he, just sitting there, might go unnoticed by a majority of the audience. There was so much action on stage maybe they wouldn't even notice a stranger sitting there; perhaps that would be even better. Maybe then I wouldn't get in so much trouble for what I was about to do.

It was then that I remembered something. I think almost every stagehand I've ever talked to can recall at least once being caught out on stage in full view of the audience for one reason or another, myself included. And what I remember is feeling a moment of real panic and the instinct to get out of view as quickly as possible. In your mind you just know every single person in that audience is looking at you and they're thinking, "Look at that dumb fucker; he stands out like a sore thumb. He's not even dressed right. Whoever he is, he's one dumb son of a bitch." So it didn't really matter if one person saw him, because I knew what he'd be thinking and that was good enough.

Just to make sure I wasn't going to get fired I told my boss, Dion, what I was planning to do and he said that if someone made a point of going to the entertainment director about this incident and if he, the director, insisted on disciplinary action, I could be issued a warning notice.

That was all I needed to hear. A little warning notice I could handle, no more than a slap on the wrist. This was great because most of the whole crew could enjoy this prank. The word went out: during the second show tomorrow night, watch number one leg after Skip's at the table. I had to let them know the joke was on Skip and I begged them not to say anything. In twenty-four hours I'd know if everyone could keep a secret.

The next night during the second show, I could hardly wait. Finally the Can-Can started and people started to gather near the rail. No, not yet! Skip wasn't on stage yet and he might sense something was up. This was too good to ruin now. Skip, however, didn't really pay attention to us and finally went on stage to wait for the dancers to come off.

Dion, my boss, showed up at the last moment and I thought, "Oh no, he's going to tell me not to do it." But that wasn't the case.

Dion said, "How can you pull the leg out and see Skip at the same time, if someone doesn't open the curtains a little for you to see?" I hadn't actually thought about not being able to see Skip, so I thanked Dion and went to stand by the line that took the leg out.

Now I had someone to tell me when Skip was in place. Standing in back of Dion were most of the crew, so my view was blocked anyway.

Dion raised his hand, then lowered it and pointed at me with a finger, the signal to go. I gave the rope one hard pull, then let it go and started toward the stage. Already, people were hooting and howling with laughter.

Skip was so amazed, and the realization of what was happening was so bizarre, that he just sat there for a couple of seconds, stunned. Just like that deer on the side of the road, hypnotized by car lights as they pass.

Then Skip went into action. Because he liked to tip back in the chair, when he started to get up real fast, he almost fell over backwards. He had to put his hand down so as not to fall onto his back. This only caused him to be on stage that much longer. He looked like a drunk who was falling out of his chair.

Finally he got to his feet, took a short bow, and walked offstage. The crew laughed about that for many years to come, Skip included.

I know that this little story about Skip doesn't involve blood or bones, but writing about him made me remember it, so before I forgot about it I thought I would tell you. And just now, another incident involving Skip comes to mind.

We have a convention area that was built at the same time as our new tower here at the Tropicana. As Stagehands, this news caught our attention because conventions, as a rule, usually involve the services of Stagehands in one capacity or another. A year later it came true.

Now, we also have what is referred to as "Slot Parties." These parties are for members who belong to the Slot Club, people who come to the Tropicana often enough to accumulate points and merchandise as a reward for playing. These people spend a lot of money here and so, three or four times a year, the hotel puts on theme parties and gives away additional cash and prizes; in fact, one year I remember them giving away a Mercedes convertible and fifty thousand dollars.

Anyway, the hotel puts a lot of effort into these parties and in their decorations to make them exciting, so that when the participants walk in they feel classy and special, which they are.

The management decided to have a Fifties theme party. The decorations would include the use of vintage classic cars of that time period. The word went out that we were to set up a stage and some of the decorations. We knew that they were looking for cars to rent for the evening. One gentleman backstage, the show's M.C. or spokesman, rented a car that he owned to the hotel. Several more cars were found; then the Vice President of Hotel Operations stepped forward and volunteered the use of his classic Plymouth. He had just completed refurbishing it at no small cost.

Our convention area is located on the second floor of the new tower, and is a good one as far as convention facilities are concerned—with one major drawback. I don't know if it was a design flaw or if the problem occurred during construction, but the outside delivery ramp, used to deliver goods and materials for the conventions that were booked in the hotel, was partially blocked by a parking spot at the bottom of the ramp. This spot was designated parking for a Vice President of the hotel. The hotel had erected a covering over the spot, six posts with a tin roof, so it was shaded during the day. This parking spot sat in front of the ramp entrance with about fifteen feet of open space between the two.

The ramp is abnormally steep, and if you believed the warnings stenciled on the retaining walls of the ramp, it couldn't even support a forklift. So for all intents and purposes, it was ineffective and probably dangerous, although it is still standing. Any truck longer than eighteen feet didn't have enough space to use the ramp. But it's been that way for fifteen years, and we've never been in a situation where we couldn't get everything we needed into the rooms, so it goes to show, where there's a will there is always a way. I didn't say we were problem-free, though.

Well, where was I? Oh yeah, Skip became involved because the classic cars were considered props, and it fell on Skip to drive the cars up the ramp, put them in the proper position, and make sure they were clean and all polished up. After the party was over, it was his job to drive the cars back down the ramp and return them to their owners. Skip by nature was very careful and always concerned about job safety, so there was no doubt that he would return the cars in perfect condition.

The only thing that could go wrong would be if there was a

problem with a car and Skip was not informed about it; like, for instance, if the car's brakes were not functioning correctly and there was a special or trick way to pump them before they worked.

The real problem was that the usual method for the cars to get into the convention area was changed a little, because Rudy, the Vice President, decided to drive his pampered prize possession up the ramp himself. More than likely, he was informed that Skip would be there later to meet the car owners, and Rudy didn't want to wait. Of course, Rudy's was the car with the bad brakes.

After the party ended, Skip began the task of driving the cars down the ramp. Finally he hopped into Rudy's car and started down. The car picked up speed at an alarming rate, due to its large size and the steep angle of the ramp. Ten feet down, Skip applied the brakes. Nothing happened.

Halfway down the ramp, the car was going about twelve miles per hour. Skip, alarmed and looking down the ramp, noticed that a car was approaching the bottom of the ramp area; he pushed the brake hard and realized it was pressed all the way down against the floorboard.

"Houston, we have a problem." Not Skip's words by any means; in fact, with the car three quarters of the way down the ramp, he was processing his options. Option one: pull the emergency brake. He did; nothing happened. Option two: pull all the way over to one side of the ramp and bail out, letting the car run wild until it hits something and comes to a stop. No, he couldn't do that because there were people walking around and more cars could pass by. Also, something could go wrong—clothing could get snagged on the car; he could trip, get run over, or be dragged screaming down the ramp.

The trucks that do manage to get up the ramp have one thing in common: all the truck drivers turn their wheels all the way to the left or right, so the truck will run against the ramp's retaining wall should the parking brake fail and the truck start to roll down the ramp. I've seen this done hundreds of times. One time I did see a truck's brake fail, and the truck rolled perhaps a foot, nudged up against the wall, and stopped, just like it was supposed to.

I'll bet Skip had seen the same thing or maybe he just thought of it on his own. Whichever was the case, that's what he did.

Since this happened at night, the sparks alone were quite a sight. Skip confirmed that the noise of concrete ripping up metal was pretty bad, too. They made those old cars really tough back then, so even though she left a trail, some fender molding, some decorative pieces, glass, and a mirror behind, the car didn't go down without a fight. Even when the left fender started to buckle and peel back, that old car was determined to reach the bottom of the ramp.

"Hold on, she's rearing to buck." I don't know what that has to do with the car, but I can almost picture Skip as a cowboy riding a wild bucking bronco. Like I said, she didn't go down without a fight, because mixed in among her body parts were a couple of big chunks of concrete, along with a lot of little chunks all over the place. Today you can still see a long scar along the wall, maybe even a little paint.

Man triumphed over machine in the end. The car fell short of the finish line, and Skip sat back and knew it had been quite a battle. I never did ask Skip if he handed Rudy the car keys personally, or how it was handled. If he did hand them over I'm sure it was special: "Rudy, on behalf of the Entertainment Department, we sincerely thank you for the use of your car. By the way, we topped off the tank for you. Thanks."

Actually, this next little story is not funny, but then again, I'm a stagehand and…well…never mind.

Part of our job is to repair or build most of what we need, and so we come in contact with many different kinds of power tools, both electric and pneumatic (air driven). As a rule, we just assume that if a guy picks up a tool, he probably knows how to use it. However, last year on Christmas Eve day my next-door neighbor, a journeyman carpenter for the last twenty years, cut his thumb off. He admitted to me that even though there was an unusual circumstance (some moisture on the piece of wood he was cutting), he was not really concentrating on cutting and was caught off guard when the saw bounced up and kicked back suddenly. Later, in the emergency room,

Tom (not Big Tom) said the nurse made the comment, "Would you happen to be a carpenter by trade, with years of experience?"

"Yes," answered Tom, feeling a little ashamed.

The nurse told him that his was the classic twenty-year injury and that the guys with years of experience should be extra careful. Nurses don't see many people with only a little experience come in with these types of injuries, because they are so concerned about getting injured.

So there are two sides to every issue, and for Bob C., I'm not sure which was the case. At the time this took place, I was on a leave of absence working on a TV series which Michael Mann was filming here in town. Bob was my replacement on the rail for the seventeen weeks I would be absent.

I met Bob on many occasions because I'd come in and visit with the guys on my lunch breaks (for two weeks we filmed right down the street from the Tropicana; then, six weeks later, we filmed at the Tropicana, so Bob and I had a chance to become acquainted with one another). He seemed to be a very quiet person, very religious, and generally well accepted by the guys on the rail, which indicated to me that he was very tolerant; if not that, then he was crazy.

Dion had high praise for Bob. "Phil, take all the time you need, we're getting along just fine here."

"Okay boss, just wanted you to know I miss you guys; this place has kind of become home to me."

Dion answered, "Well then, don't forget to write home." It was nice to know I was missed, too.

Toward the end of my leave of absence, Dion would greet me with, "Does security know you're on the property?" Or, "It's a shame there's not a position open; I hate to see Bob go."

I thought to myself, "Yeah, but look what you're getting in return, your old trusted servant."

Ah, Dion was just kidding with me, even though I heard how Bob was flawless; Bob was this; Bob did that. Shit, I was beginning to dislike Bob very much, even though it wasn't his fault for doing his best, which everyone should do anyway. Still, at the time I began to feel a little threatened by Bob.

Finally the TV series was completed. Mr. Mann footed the bill for the wrap party (the party thrown by the production company at the end of filming). It was very classy; some people would say, "First cabin, all the way." Thank you very much. The following evening I decided to pop into the Trop real fast and confirm with Dion that my work was finished and find out when he would schedule me back to work.

Dion told me, "What's the matter with you? You just got done working seventeen weeks, six and seven days a week, and I know those days were no shorter than thirteen hour days. So that's what? Something like forty-two, forty-three thousand dollars the last four months? Why don't you take a little time off, take your wife on a vacation, rest up a little if nothing else. I got you covered; go home, spend some money. Then come back in a week and we'll talk about getting you back on the schedule."

Now I was getting a little annoyed. What did he mean by "We'll talk about getting you back on the schedule"? Shit, I'm on the schedule buddy, so don't think otherwise. My mind also told me that if Dion really wanted to replace me, even though I was an A-list card-carrying member, he could choose any number of methods, and if he chose to vigorously pursue those methods, I would be out of a job. So, being that money wasn't a big concern at the moment, I decided to keep my mouth shut and make a wise decision by retreating gracefully and going home.

It turned out that Dion's advice had some merit to it. Once I finally relaxed I slept for two days straight; I was exhausted. The next couple of days my wife and I discussed what kind of furniture we should buy for our house, which we had just bought eight months earlier. We could even spend a little money on ourselves if we chose to; however, I didn't tell my wife about my fears of not being invited back to work.

Enough of that; I could worry all I wanted to later. For the next couple of days I was just going to relax. Fuck work.

I was finally relaxed and was making plans with my family when the phone rang. I answered the phone and to my surprise, it was Dion.

"What's up Dion, you changed your mind, now you miss me so much you had to call and say hello?" There you go, asshole, and if it's a favor you're asking, let me think about it for a week, then you come back and see me; then we'll discuss if I can help you out or not. That's what my head was telling me to say.

"Phil, come in tonight on your same set of cues. You still remember them, right?" asked Dion.

"Yeah, I remember. So what happened? Did the new guy die or something? Maybe he missed a cue; yeah, that's it, he fucked up royally, I bet."

"Are you going to be here? Yes or no?"

"Okay Dion, you know you can count on me if I say I'll be there, so I'll be there."

"See ya," he said.

But before he could hang up I said, "Dion, it seems to me something's going on that's more serious than you care to discuss with me at the moment, but is there anything that I can do?"

"Yeah, show up, you're back on the schedule. 'Bye." Dion was off the phone.

Damn, would I be the ass if what I predicted was the case. Since Dion was never one for explanations, it would have been a wasted effort even if I would have had time to ask him on the phone. Jeez, should I wear my Sunday best, just in case?

I headed into work, and entering the backstage doors I had the odd sensation of almost being a stranger. It could have been due to the fact that during my leave a couple of new guys had been hired. At first, the new faces threw me off a little.

As usual, the guys were sitting around the card table laughing and carrying on like always. They didn't look like anyone died. But then again, nothing on the rail was sacred; we joked about anything and everything. For example, after my father passed away, I took off a couple of days from work. I went over to see my mother; all of a sudden her husband and best friend was gone, and I knew the first few nights would be unbearable and I didn't want her to be alone. When I got back to work, many expressed their condolences but one of the guys asked me, "Hey, Phil, does this mean you're homeless now?" It was beautiful; it made me laugh a little, and it was okay. Another thing, if you dished out the bullshit, you damn sure better be able to take it.

"What happened to Bob?" I asked. "Dion didn't tell me anything earlier."

We had two Toms on the rail and they happen to be brothers-in-law. It was Tom F. who answered. "He almost shot himself in the dick with a staple gun."

"Hell," I said. "What a puss; I've got a set of Little Scholar junior tools; they even make sounds like real tools."

"Phil, he shot himself with a pneumatic gun; you know, with 90 pounds of pressure. He tried to pull the staple out with a pair of pliers, but it was into the bone too deep."

Gee, Bob was turning out to be a lot tougher than I gave him credit for; maybe I'll take back that wisecrack about the little tools. That sounded nasty; it sounded worse than the two guys I knew who worked in a scenery shop. They had worked around the clock to get the show finished in time and were a half hour away from being finished. All they had to do was screw in a couple of pieces of Masonite onto a set piece. To make things easier, one guy stood in back and made sure the guidelines didn't move, while the guy in front drove the screws in. The one in back put his hand against the Masonite for just a second and was resting his head on his arm. The guy in front missed the mark and drove a two and ¾ inch needle-nose screw through the 3/8-inch Masonite and through the other guy's hand. Hearing the screams, he ran around to the back of the set to see what the hell was happening. Meanwhile, his friend was still screwed to the set. As soon as he realized what had happened, the first guy ran to the front again and backed the screw out, which was almost as painful as it was going in.

But I don't think that's as bad as a one and 1/3 inch L-model staple pushed into your bones by 90 pounds of air, and if you think ninety pounds may not sound like that much, you have to consider that there is a ratio involved. I couldn't tell you what it is, but if you convert the pounds into miles per hour or feet per second that the staple travels, it's probably pretty impressive.

Anyway, Bob had been working on some project backstage and had to climb a ladder to staple up high. These guns have a safety that's seated in front of the barrel of the gun. You can't shoot any staples if the safety bar is not pushed in; in other words, you have to press the barrel of the gun down against your material, so the bar is pushed in also. It's a good safety system and has prevented many accidents.

Bob, however, beat the system. He seemed to have made the mistake of having his finger on the trigger while climbing up the ladder. His movements were such that when he lifted one hand to the next rung of the ladder, the hand holding the gun was accidentally jammed into his upper thigh. The gun performed as it should, except that the barrel wasn't against any material, but rather against human flesh and bones.

At one point in my working life I had accepted some day work at a scenery shop, employed as a painter. As time went by, I observed who I thought were the best carpenters. Slowly I began to hand them their tools or materials, being helpful without getting in their way. In return they started to explain to me what they were doing and why they were doing it. Although I wasn't much of a carpenter when I left the shop, I could at least read a tape measure.

One day while we were working in the shop, a bad thunderstorm developed and one of the lightning strikes hit a transformer nearby, causing our power to go out. We were just about ready to go to lunch. Since we had no power, the foreman told us to wash up and take our lunch a little early.

When we came back to the shop an hour later the power was still off, so we gathered near the roll-up doors and sat on or near a set piece that was being sanded in preparation for a paint job. Just like the rest of us, the gentleman using the belt sander when the power went out simply set the sander down on the set piece, and was waiting for the power to come back on. We were having a good time bullshitting with each other, telling a bunch of lies. A couple of guys had grabbed some old packing blankets and laid them out on the floor to relax on.

Suddenly the lights popped on and the whole shop seemed to come to life on its own. Saws started up, compressors began to hum, and things started to move. One guy had been using a jigsaw when the power went out. He had just let it sit on the material and waited for the power to come back.

In the area where we were gathered, the belt sander hummed to life and shot forward, flying off the set piece. Bill C. was lying on the floor on the packing blanket a few feet away when the belt sander crashed into his forehead, ripping his glasses from his face. The 80-grit sandpaper did a quick polish job on his nose before running out of cord and dying a sudden death.

Just about everyone who was using power tools that day made the same mistake: when the power went out, we just set our tools down. If you had the "hold power" button engaged and didn't release it, when the power came back on the tool started operating at maximum power.

Thank God Bill wasn't hurt bad; a headache and a bright red nose and, oh yeah, he received twelve stitches in his head. The scab on his nose looked pretty funny. Bill told me that perhaps if he hadn't had his glasses on, he might have inured his eyes.

My role at the shop as a painter sometimes left me with time on my hands. Until something was built, I didn't have anything to do. So sometimes I'd offer my services to the carpenters, and many times they'd say it would be a big help if I could work on their cut list (a list of what materials needed to be cut, lengths, widths, etc.). By doing that, I freed them from that boring task and allowed them to begin the task of doing their layout.

I volunteered one time when a job came in that was particularly large. Given the list of materials to cut, it was clear that this was going to be a two or thee day job. Maybe it's just me, but the sound of a table saw, that continuous high-pitched whine, combined with the hours you stand there working it…well, I find it slightly hypnotizing. A certain rhythm is developed. If you have to cut two hundred 4x8 sheets of plywood down to 3'6" x 8', you start to handle and cut the wood in a routine that's easiest for you to do. After a couple of hours, it's easy to find yourself daydreaming—a dangerous state of mind to be in when you're working with a piece of machinery that can eliminate your fingers or a whole hand in less than a second.

The second day after lunch I was back behind the saw working, but thinking about this new girl I was taking out to dinner that evening. I had the uncut lumber on the left, and after the cut was made, I would stack it to the right of the saw, then reach back over with my right hand (over the top of the blade) and pick up another piece to cut. Reaching for another piece, I heard the slightest change in the whining pitch of the saw, and at the same instant, felt a sharp tug on one finger.

Instinctively I jerked my hand back and grabbed it with my other hand, as if that would keep my fingers from falling off. After a second, panic started to fill my head. Oh God, I sure don't want to lose my fingers. I knew from experience that it's not uncommon for people to run with no particular destination; just run, because the mind is so overwhelmed that the body functions on its own and running is what it will sometimes choose to do. That's what my body started to do.

Thank God one of the guys just happened to be watching me, or maybe he saw a jerking movement out of the corner of his eye. In any event, Russ was standing next to me like he materialized out of thin air. He grabbed my arm with one hand and put his other hand over mine. "Phil, I'm gonna walk you over to a chair and we'll see how bad it is, but I promise you everything will be all right," he said. "That's it, big guy, we're almost there."

I didn't even answer him, and felt like maybe I was going to pass out. I do remember thinking, "Where's all the blood?" I had learned in my paramedic training that traumatic amputation caused the veins and arteries to restrict (close off), a defense mechanism the body uses in this situation. Even then, there's still a good amount of blood.

Russ knelt down before me and said, "Let go of your hand. We need to take a quick look and then get it wrapped up. Hold your arm up."

"God, Russ, I can't look, I just can't."

"Phil, I can see all your fingertips, so at least they're still attached. Come on, let go."

So I released my grip and let Russ examine me. He looked at one side, then turned my hand over and checked it out. Now the pain was starting to creep in, and more fear. How was I going to pull ropes, do anything, without fingers?

Russ let out a little chuckle and shoved my hand away. "Look," he said.

"No. I think I'm going to be sick."

"Look you big baby, you're okay," Russ said, laughing louder now.

"Oh sure, it's easy for you to say I'm fine, when you still have all your digits."

"Hey guys, come over and see the mighty wound that the painter has."

Slowly I looked down at my mangled hand, ready to accept the pity and concern that would be given me because of the sad condition my body was now in.

Fingers were all there, nothing dangling. They moved all right. There! It was blood, but it was dried blood. What was going on? I knew I had felt the blade hit my hand; I'd felt the tug on my fingers, but there they were. But I was starting to feel unbelievable pain; I mean it was just starting to build up; I knew it was going to be bad and I was getting faint; I was just about ready to pass out. So I couldn't be all right!

But lo and behold, everything was there. I then turned my still-shaking hand over, and on the bottom of two fingers were the same identical small nicks, with a little dried blood.

Now I was starting to laugh with the others, laughing so hard I had tears in my eyes; I don't know, maybe I was really crying.

Later Russ came up to me and said, "It's all right to get a little scared after something like that happens." And fortunately for me, I had just learned a lesson that other guys have paid a much deeper price to learn.

Years later, Russ bounced into the Trop for a rail call and it was impossible to ignore the long, jagged scar that started along the side of his neck, went up along one cheek, and disappeared into his hair in the temple area of his head. Later that night, he explained to me what had happened.

He had been cutting steel all day on a TCD saw and had just put a new blade in and resumed cutting. These metal cutting blades are a little unusual in several ways. First, they're large, round disks; the one Russ was cutting with was a 14 inch blade, and if you weren't acquainted with the construction business, you might not guess that this disk would be used for cutting steel.

The second unusual thing is that the blade is fragile; if you drop one, there is a good chance it will shatter, which I always thought was strange because it did cut through steel easily. At first, I mistakenly thought that to cut through steel, the blade would have to be harder and stronger. Like in life, what you sometimes assume to be true and logical is just a misconception.

When you're operating this type of saw, the manual states in bold letters: "Warning! Blades may shatter. Continue to hold the operating handle in the down position if this occurs."

I've had them shatter on me once or twice and it scared the shit out of me. It's a loud, sudden bang, and even though there is a safety cover over the blade, pieces can still fly out from the bottom of the saw. Now maybe I'm just a jumpy sort of fellow, but my first instinct is to let the handle go and get the hell out of there, which is the opposite of what I should do.

I knew Russ' work ethics so there's no doubt at all that he was wearing all safety equipment. Accidents happen and this one was a freak accident, it's as simple as that.

Russ was cutting, the blade shattered, and a piece ricocheted off something and traveled back toward his face. Russ was wearing a plastic face shield but it was a one in a million shot. The blade piece hit Russ in the cheek between his face and the safety shield, and traveled upward along his face and head before stopping.

Russ required hundreds of stitches, eye surgery, and other operations to repair the muscles in his cheeks and mouth, then months of rehabilitation to get everything back to normal as much as possible.

Russ said to me, "All those years that I treated tools with respect, wore every goddamn piece of safety equipment you can imagine, no matter how careful I was, this still happened. Well, at least I've still got all my fingers and toes, thank God."

Two months later he lost three fingers. No, I'm just kidding with you. And don't say, "Hey, that's not even funny," because to a real stagehand, it would be. I love ya, Russ.

Since this chapter is called "Broken Bones and Blood," if you'll bear with me a while longer, we'll get into the real meat and potatoes, the heart of the matter. The real crazy stuff. The main reason I am writing this stuff is because I've been told too many times that this is what movies are made of. I'm not sure about that, but I do know that the entertainment industry seems to provide tremendous opportunities for mistakes and other things to happen that are not only very funny, but are also unusual. And it also seems that the people drawn into this industry are even wackier than the things that happen to them. I simply do not have the imagination to create such stories; it would be hard for even the most creative person. So if you can, imagine the feelings you'd have if you had to walk in our shoes—when a mistake we make causes a show to stop, scenery to be destroyed, or animals to run away. Just put yourself in our place.

I had the good fortune of being employed by a number of production companies during the 1980's. Previously I had been an ambulance driver/attendant, and prior to that I worked in the emergency room at a hospital called Southern Nevada Memorial Hospital, later renamed University Medical Center, or UMC. It was around that same time that the paramedic program came into existence, and it became obvious that to continue in the ambulance business, I would have to get certified. One of the physicians I knew and respected offered to pay all expenses if I would commit to the six months' training period. If I quit (not failed, but quit), not only would I have to pay him back with interest, but also on the side window of my car, he would take soap and write, "I'm a quitter," every chance he got. So I accepted his offer, and six months later I was a paramedic.

When I left the medical field for stage work, I kept up my certifications just in case things didn't work out. That was a good thing.

Probably because we used people from the Union Hall as extras backstage, word of my medical experience reached back to the Hall. It was a time when the motion picture industry was coming to Nevada much more frequently. Fewer permits were needed than in California; it was rumored that there were fewer hassles, fewer union difficulties, and that costs were lower.

Whatever the reasons, the state of Nevada and especially our Union, Local 720, The International Alliance of Theatrical Stage Employees and Moving Picture Machine Operators of the United States and Canada (I always liked the sound of that; I couldn't pronounce half of those words to begin with, but when someone else said them, it sounded impressive), were waiting with open arms.

As a Union, the majority of our work was generated by the showrooms and conventions booked by the convention areas. We also had some people who were camera operators and assistants, plus a few other people who had a working knowledge of the motion picture industry.

Soon that was to change. Educational classes were conducted at the Hall, and more and more qualified people followed the industry into Nevada and into our local. It was the Union's goal to have the Nevada area fall under Local 720's jurisdiction. We finally won the argument over jurisdiction after many years of California's IATSE Local claiming that Nevada fell into its jurisdiction.

After Nevada's Local won jurisdiction over Nevada workers, our Local 720 was in the process of tying up a few organizational loose ends. One was the First Aid and Medical Craft Division, which supplied medical services directly to the set or location. Lawmakers had recently required this practice as a condition for filming in Nevada.

I became the first person in our Local to hold that position, and it was a wonderful experience. A fantastic experience.

The first two or three movies that I worked on were easy and uneventful. I never thought I would ever get close to any of the principals (main stars), but luckily I was mistaken.

Vitamin shots—that's right, that was the item that opened the door, and I'm talking literally. It seemed that in California the principals were requesting and receiving vitamin shots, the most common being vitamin B12, on a frequent basis. The stars didn't come to you; you came to them. I was making house calls or, more correctly, trailer calls.

This practice would continue on every project I did. It became an invitation, once I got to know the principals. On one particular movie set the leading man would get upset and ask if I was okay, if I didn't have breakfast with him. (No, it wasn't a gay thing.)

Anyway, as I was saying, the first two movies went pretty smoothly—a couple of sprained body parts, a few minor cuts, and that was about it. Then I was hired to do "Crime Story." This was a major television series, and the cast and crew could number in the hundreds. I thought it would be just what I needed, a challenge. I said a challenge, not an ordeal.

I reported to the production office on a Monday morning at 5:30. I was loaded down with a ton of equipment, with still more to be delivered to the film site. We were to be transported to the sites daily.

"Excuse me," I asked one of the production assistants, or P.A.'s, "but all my equipment can't possibly fit in this van; how will it get to the site?"

"Oh, uh, we'll load it on another van and get it out to you right away," he said.

"Well, okay, I guess that's all right." I grabbed a few bags that were essential and left the rest in the care of the P.A. I don't remember if I had identified myself or not, but if I hadn't, it would be a big mistake.

That first day was not so bad, except that by noon the rest of my equipment had not yet arrived. No big deal, I guess, what could happen the first day? I reasoned with myself.

It was 5:30 p.m. and I had just been told that we were packing up and moving down the road to a topless club, rented by our production group for the evening. They gave me a condensed script so I would know what type of physical action was to be performed—fights, car scenes, whatever. I had requested such a list so I could better prepare for possible safety and medical problems that might present themselves.

The scene coming up would involve three stunt men, a shootout scene, and a guy being beaten up, about what you'd expect in a TV episode. The club, known as the Pussycat-A-Go-Go, was the real deal. It had two parking lots, one in back and one to the side of the building. When we arrived the trucks, vans, and almost everyone were clumped in the side lot. Before filming continued, we took a dinner break.

"Time to roll!" yelled the Second A.D. (Assistant Director), so off to work they went. At the back of the prop truck, the Property Master was checking and then loading the guns to be used, with blanks in the chambers. I suddenly recollected a story about an actor who had been killed when a wad from a blank hit his temple, killing him.

My equipment still hadn't caught up with us yet; however, we were a couple of hours from a wrap for the day, so I wasn't too worried. As I walked by the prop truck, the driver asked if I wanted to relax, and motioned to a folding chair. I thanked him and set my bags down next to the truck. The driver, Jerry, was a Teamster who made his home in Canada.

He had just given me a Coke when over the radio came a frantic shout for assistance: "Help! Oh God, oh God, no! No." Then silence.

I was up in a flash, my radio in hand. "Who is this? What is your location please?" No response. Had to be in the club, I guessed. I grabbed my meager bags of supplies and headed toward the building.

"The gunfight," I thought. "Somebody got hit by a wad." I was mentally kicking myself in the ass for letting my equipment get away from me.

As I neared the corner of the building I heard someone yelling, "Medic!" I turned and answered; in a second, I was standing in front of a very upset Teamster. He told me that a fellow Teamster (Teamsters were responsible for all transportation) had been shot by another not-so-fellow Teamster, two or possibly three times.

"Shit, okay, tell me where the gun is, first," I said.

"The gun?"

"Yeah, where's the shooter, the gun?"

"I don't know. Come on!"

This was not good, not good at all. It wouldn't do anyone any good if the medic or anyone else was taken down because the shooter was still running around popping people. However, I had to weigh that against the man who was lying on the ground nearby with his life draining away while I battled with this dilemma. Help the guy, take the chance, keep your eyes open; it's the only thing you can do—oh, and pray.

The Teamster led me to the place where the young man lay bleeding. I stopped by the corner of a parked van and took a quick glance around. People were starting to gather around; it was impossible to tell if one of them was the guy I was afraid of. Shit, well, got to do it now. I walked quickly to the stricken man, knelt down and said, "If you can hear me, you can send me a thank you note later, because you're not going to die."

With ninety percent of my equipment missing, I had to make do with what I had and pray for the rest. Check breathing…breathing shallow with intermittent coughing; frothy blood exiting mouth. Control the bleeding. I did a quick exam and located the entrance wounds. I cut open the shirt, exposed the chest, and there they were: two little pencil-sized holes in the upper chest area. I didn't have my stethoscope or blood pressure cuff, but I didn't really need them; I knew immediately that if I didn't seal the wounds, the blood filling his lungs would drown him anyway. I had to seal up this sucking chest wound.

I took out my pack of cigarettes and started to remove the cellophane. "Christ, Doc, what are you gonna do, stop and take a cigarette break?" someone screamed at me.

"Do you smoke?" I yelled.

"WHAT?"

"If you smoke, give me the cellophane. I need three more pieces," I said. "I don't have time to explain, but this guy's life depends on it, so go!"

That guy didn't screw around; he was back in no time. I got the man into a sitting position and asked for two volunteers, and they came quickly.

"I'm going to put a cellophane piece over each hole; you guys hold them in place. If you don't, he'll die." I reached into my bag and got a small canister of oxygen and a couple of other things.

It just so happened that the young man who'd been shot was the son of the head Teamster on the job. It was about this same time that his father showed up after being told of the incident. He came screaming up to us in a station wagon and parked right next to us. "Put him in the car! I'm taking him to the hospital."

By now there were ten or so big Teamsters around me, with a couple of them already stepping over to lift his son. When I stood up to listen to the father, his car doors were open and there, stacked in the rear of the station wagon, was all my equipment! I tried to tell him that his son stood a much better chance with me because I could now stabilize him while waiting for the ambulance. But the man had made up his mind that he was taking his son to the hospital and no one, especially some young kid, was going to stop him.

"Let me put some oxygen on him and I'll go with you," I said. I put the mask on his son and ran around to the other side to get my bags. When I threw my bags into the back seat, I caught a glimpse into the rear storage area of the wagon holding all the rest of my equipment. Evidently the Teamster boss had been driving around with it all day.

I shut the door and ran back to where the O2 bottle was sitting on the ground. I was going to put the bottle in the car, hop in next to the injured man, and off we'd go. But before I got there, I heard a door slam shut and the car tore off into the night. I was left standing there with the O2 bottle, and as the car drove off I saw the O2 line flapping around outside the closed door of the wagon.

Not only did that whole exercise in emergency medicine go

terribly wrong, but now I was standing in the parking lot with a penlight, scissors, and a bottle of oxygen. I didn't so much as have a Band-Aid on me, and all of my equipment was in the station wagon.

Finally that first day ended. Two weeks later, the young man went home from the hospital. I guess the head Teamster put the word out that I was to be given Carte Blanche as far as their services could be extended. Also, we had a meeting to get our priorities straight.

During the midway point of the series a guy from Los Angeles joined the film crew. I'm not sure of his title, but after the cameraman would change the film in the camera he'd hand it to this guy, who would take it somewhere to be stored until the end of the day.

I try not to judge people but this guy had a real attitude. He was hot shit, knew it all and was, in his own mind, the funniest son of a bitch on the planet. This player of practical jokes soon put himself at the top of everyone's shit list.

One day he'd just taken possession of a film canister and, while fooling around, dropped the can. It bounced down a little ravine and the can opened; I assume the film was ruined. Although this cooled his jets a bit, it wasn't long before he returned to his usual self. A friend of mine has told me many times that the human ego has the fastest recuperative power known to man. I believe him.

One day this clown was fooling around with one of the cameramen; he had a razor knife and was pretending to slash the other fellow. The cameraman got tired of the guy and ignored him and started to walk away. Funny Boy made one last slash with the knife, only this time he did it by pressing the knife against the cameraman's shirt. His supposedly make-believe slash started high on the left shoulder, continued down across the back, and onto the rear right hip.

If you've ever used razor knives, you know that every once in a while, whether it's because the blades are seated wrong, the knife holder has been damaged on the end, or a blade is an odd length— whatever the reason—the blades are not always fully retracted. And on this day, a good 1/8-inch of blade was still unsheathed. Before my very eyes, and those of Mr. Joker, the cameraman's shirt fell open and his back parted like the Red Sea.

Mr. Funny Guy stood there gasping at the destruction he'd just caused, then fainted dead away. Meanwhile the cameraman, who had a good idea of what had just been done to him, sat calmly down on a rock.

"I knew that little fuck was gonna hurt somebody; I just knew it. I've been trying to stay away from him from the moment he got here. How bad is it?"

"Well," I said, "If it was your face, you'd never be in the movies again. It's a strange wound; it's deep enough for stitches in some areas, but not in others. Give me a minute and I'm going to wrap you up tighter than a tamale."

One thing I always carried with me was a box of tampons. If you consider their use, and the fact that they're sterile, it's no surprise that they can have many uses. Now was one of those times. But I didn't tell him what I was using; I just started to lay those babies against the cut. As soon as a little blood soaked in, they stayed right in place. Beautiful. I then wrapped his torso and he was ready to go. He wondered why he could hear little snickers behind his back when this really wasn't funny at all.

He was back the next day and looked me up at lunchtime. "Thank you very much for your help and expertise. Oh, by the way, I didn't want you to run out of these." He tossed a new box of tampons on the table and it took even me by surprise. Now everyone around started laughing and looking at me. Very funny. I like this guy!

While working as a spotlight operator, I was at a hotel show which featured horses harnessed to chariots. They ran on large treadmills, like a scene from the movie "Ben Hur." One of the treadmills broke down, sending the horse, chariot, and rider into the audience. I can't remember the number of people injured but for a minute, we all thought it was part of the show.

One friend got too close to a tiger: 144 stitches.

Another friend was hit in the face by a piece of plywood that fell sixty feet from a grid; it chopped his nose off.

People get run over by pieces of scenery.

And I'm sure there are accidents that I've forgotten about or didn't hear about. This is a fantastic industry to work in, but because of the complexities of bringing live entertainment to an audience, or with all the stunts and special effects we've come to expect from the movies, accidents will continue to happen.

CHAPTER 9

HEY, THAT COULD HAVE BEEN A DISASTER

One gentleman who passed through the rail department at the Tropicana was someone whom I greatly admired, not because of the antics I am going to write about, but because of what he accomplished during the last two years of his life.

Jack was as a character, no doubt about it. I had met him back when I was in high school, where his son and I played sports together; he would attend the games. He was older than the rest of us on the rail by twenty years or so, but he was a practical joker, and although his drug of choice was alcohol, he fit in quite nicely with the rest of us.

There was one big difference: Jack owned his own airplane and to this day, despite the lack of good judgement on his part, I believe that his skills as a pilot were very good.

When the subject of flying came up one evening and we found out just what Jack did as a hobby, we quickly had him agreeing to take us flying. What better time to go than after the second show? We would all be feeling pretty good by then, plus Jack would have a good buzz on too, so we set a date for a couple of nights later for our first flight.

Jack had acquired a small portion of a hanger, large enough for his plane, a bathroom, desk, small refrigerator, and his tools. It was rumored that he was going through a divorce at the time, and that perhaps the hanger was his temporary living quarters also.

I've got to tell you, we were all pretty excited; when the second show finally ended that evening, we were ready to go flying. After the show we piled into Jack's Cadillac and headed out to his hangar.

The plane was nothing special to look at, all aluminum with one prop, but despite its common looks its structural properties were very impressive. Based on the things Jack did with that plane, I'd have to believe it.

"Come on, we have to push the plane out of the hangar; after that, we all pile in and buckle up." We taxied to the runway and waited for the tower to give us permission to take off. Permission granted. Three minutes later we were making a slow, lazy turn over the lights of Las Vegas.

I like flying. Clear weather, stormy, in the clouds, whatever—I would have flown with a blind man just to get off the ground. Well, in a way, we were flying with a blind man.

Jack flew us over the city for about twenty minutes; then he said, "Hey, Phil, where do you live?"

"Over by Western High School," I answered.

"When we get near your house, point it out to me, will you?"

So I did and Jack said, "Hang on." He made a wide circle, all the while gaining altitude and then, when he had my house lined up, went into a steep dive. He buzzed my house, so low that you could have read the street sign if it had been daylight. As I looked back at my house, lights were coming on all over the neighborhood. "Jesus H. Christ, Jack, you crazy bastard, how low did you go?"

"The instruments say about fifty feet, but they may be off a little. I'd say it was closer to forty or forty-five feet from ground level."

No wonder lights were coming on. At three o'clock in the morning, it had to sound like a freight train was coming through their homes.

Jack proceeded to do that with the other two guys' homes; then, as a final act, he flew up Charleston Road at maybe thirty feet above the power lines. When we passed the last homes he pulled up, flew toward the mountains, and then slowly turned back to the airport. Right before we landed Jack said, "Oh, listen guys, I need you to maybe do me a favor."

"Sure!" we all said at once.

Jack said, "If by some chance after we've landed we get a visit from an F.A.A. official, tell him we've been flying out over the Lake Mead area and just flew in from the east. It seems there have been a couple of complaints about a low-flying airplane in the valley area, but no one could give a description because it was too dark. I assured them it couldn't possibly have been us, because we were in another area."

No problem; we would have sworn we were at the lake, but no one ever asked. He was off the hook.

Weeks later we were off on another early morning outing; this time we didn't press our luck as far as the house buzzing was concerned. No, we were in for a whole new experience.

"You guys ever hear of a Shandale?" (I don't even know how to spell this word.)

"No," we answered.

He pulled the airplane nose straight up and for the next twenty seconds or so, we were staring out the windshield up at the stars.

Soon the engine started to sputter and then died altogether.

"Fuck! What's going on? You didn't tell us about this engine quitting. Shit!"

The plane made a lazy turn on its left side, the nose pointing back to earth. Now we were plummeting toward the ground. It was deathly quiet, with only the rush of the wind sweeping over the airplane. What seemed like a long time was probably only seconds before the engine started to sputter and cough, finally starting up again. Wow, what a rush!

"Does that happen every time you do that?" I asked.

"I hope so," was all he said. He took us through a couple more maneuvers before we headed back in. He had us hooked. We wanted to go up whenever he'd take us.

One night we received an unexpected check from some filming that had taken place in our showroom.

"Hey, Jack, let's go flying after the show. How about it?"

"Sure, sounds like fun," Jack said.

After the show we went to the Holiday Casino, cashed our checks, gambled, drank, and continued to get more blasted. About 3:00 a.m. we headed over to the hangar. On the way we picked up a couple of bottles of Chivas Regal. We still had six or seven excellent joints of weed left for the flight.

Somehow we decided that breakfast in Bull Head, Arizona (about two hours away) would be neat, then fly home; we'd be back about 8:30 the next morning.

We went through the usual routine of pushing the plane out of the hangar. Everyone climbed in and we were ready to go.

"We need gas," Jack said. We all climbed out while Jack and Bob went to order gas. Driving in Jack's car, they went to a building where they operated a combination lock allowing them to enter, and then placed their gas order.

As Jack and Bob returned to the plane, I was standing there watching. It's true that I didn't know the airport layout well, but I could have sworn they'd just driven across a runway that a plane took off from a couple of minutes earlier. No, I had to be wrong; I mean, a person would have to be pretty fucked up to drive across the airport runway, right? Right.

Once again we all got into the plane. Jack was pushing buttons and flipping switches but nothing happened. "Shit, the battery's dead. I'll have to call for a jump."

Again we all piled out and stood around waiting for the truck to come and jump the battery. This was a big truck with a giant generator mounted on the back.

The driver pulled up to the side of the plane, hopped out, and dragged a couple of 50-amp cables over to the plane. As soon as the second cable was attached he went back to the plane and started the generator. Jack had forgotten to shut everything down, so as soon as the power started to flow, the plane started right up.

The guy started screaming, "Shut the fucking plane down! Shut it down!"

Jack said, "Okay, shut up, the plane's off, you dick."

Now the guy disconnected the cables, all the while calling Jack every name in the book.

Jack told us later, "I guess the guy had a right to be pissed. We dragged his truck about 15 feet or so. It's the prop starting up like that which scared him." So that's why his last act before driving away was to give us the bird.

This time, nothing was going to stop us; we were on our way. We taxied down to the runway and sat there. Jack fumbled with the radio. I noticed a plane behind us, but still we sat there; the plane went around us and took off. Then another plane did the same. Shit, what is this? Did they take a number before us, or something?

"Jack, what's up? How come these planes are taking off before us?" we asked.

"I'm having a little problem. I'm having trouble dialing into the tower; can you read the numbers on the radio?" Damn, maybe that was not a good sign.

I read Jack the numbers and soon he was talking with the tower. "Hold on guys, they want us to hold for a minute before they give us clearance."

I don't know where these guys all came from so quickly but we were surrounded, worse than Custer was at Bull Run. Airport Security and Metro Police had us pinned in very nicely. "Everyone please come down out of the plane—now."

"Jack, shut it down, we're not flying tonight," I said.

Jack shut the plane off. One by one we got out of the plane, but not before Allen first swallowed all the joints. However, the two bottles of Chivas Regal were still on the plane in a small cooler. A spokesman for the small army of police and security forces stepped up to question us.

"Where in hell do you think you guys were going? Who's the pilot of this plane?"

"Jack's my goddamn name. Who the fuck are you?" Wow Jack, don't do this. I put my hands out, wrists together, and held them in front of the Metro officer nearest to me.

"What are you doing?" he asked me.

"Put the cuffs on, I know we're going to jail. I just know it. By the way, I'll tell you whatever you want to know." I'll sing like a bird, I thought.

"Put your hands down, you ass, you're not in trouble here—yet," Metro answered. Okay.

Mr. Spokesman was really very cool; he put up with one very drunk and obnoxious pilot and was getting little or no cooperation, so he tried a different tactic.

"Listen fellows, it's quite evident your friend here is pretty well out of it. Could you persuade him to allow us to take his plane back to his hangar? We'll lock everything up and then sometime tomorrow, if he'll contact us, we'll see if we can't come to a solution that will be agreeable to all parties. Perhaps this situation will not get blown all out of proportion, if you get my meaning."

This guy was very cool and he was more than fair. "Let us talk with Jack for a moment, okay?"

"Sure, fellows, take a minute."

We pushed Jack a few feet away and told him what Mr. F.A.A. had told us.

"NO ONE'S GOING TO TOUCH MY FUCKING AIRPLA...

Allen got his hand over Jack's mouth. "He says that will be fine."

"Good, now get him out of here and we'll take care of the rest."

We pulled Jack to the Cadillac and he started to settle down. Just as he started to get behind the wheel, Bob grabbed him and tossed him into the back seat. Metro gave us a thumbs-up.

As we were driving away, we stopped by the plane. It had occurred to us that the cooler was still on the plane, so what difference did it make if we asked for it back?

They gave it to us; so you see, it never hurts to ask. Then, back in the car, Allen said, "God, it's a good thing we left. I don't think my legs can hold me up any longer."

"Ah, ya pussy, you were that scared?" we joked.

"No, I ate those six joints and they're really starting to kick my ass. I'm really getting loaded; that's what I mean," he said. The jerk, he went and did all the pot; now we didn't have any, the bogart!

Supposedly Jack had a heart problem, possibly related to his drinking. I'm not sure. Anyway, after that last little incident at the airport—well, we were grounded. Jack left the rail soon after that, and a year passed before his name surfaced again.

Jack was flying again, and one day he took another stagehand, Dana P., up for an afternoon of fun in the skies. There was a mild breeze that day, and soon they had left the valley behind. Their destination was Lake Mead, where nude sunbathing was a common practice on the boats. It was fun buzzing the boats and checking out the young hard, naked bodies.

One particular boat caught their attention. Naked sunbathers waved to them on their first pass. This must have been special, because Jack buzzed them again. This time they sort of waved them away; once was fine, twice was enough.

Over the lake, the breeze was a little stronger, producing small waves crested with white caps. Jack decided to make one more pass, a low pass to really buzz them good. Plus, Jack knew that the people on the boat were a little annoyed already. Fuck 'em if they couldn't take a joke.

Jack came in fast and low, sailing over the top of the boat with clearance measured in a matter of feet. As they looked back, they saw a couple of bathers flip them the bird.

Jack looked forward again and instantly knew he was in trouble. The plane was much too low, almost touching the water. Reacting, he pulled up hard—too hard. The tail of the plane was forced down into the water. The sudden drag overpowered the pull of the engine, at the same time reducing his airspeed by more than half.

The plane was doomed, its only course of action being to flop hard into the water. In a matter of minutes it was resting on the floor of Lake Mead. By Jack's estimate, it was close to a hundred feet down. And that's where it remains to this day.

Forgetting their earlier displeasure at having their privacy invaded, the sunbathers with their boat were there to rescue the two airmen almost immediately. If nothing else, Jack and Dana were very lucky people; no injuries to speak of except a very bruised ego.

Something happened to Jack, something personal in his life. He quit drinking. When I talked to his son John, I could tell that Jack was having an impact on his family; his reputation around the Union Hall had also improved considerably.

One time while talking to John, I learned things about Jack that were pretty amazing. He put his kids through private Catholic schools, both elementary and high school, and on into college. He provided his family with a comfortable lifestyle and a nice home. Jack took a personal interest in his family that was to be commended, despite his drinking.

Jack is one of the individuals who hold a seat in the "Stagehands Hall of Fame."

One night during the first show, the rail phone rang and it was the Union Hall on the line. They were very sorry to inform us that Jack Dider was killed earlier that evening, when the car he was driving was extensively damaged as it passed through an intersection in town. He had been hit by a drunk driver and died instantly. End of story.

I think of you often, Jack, and have said quite a few prayers on your behalf, although you probably didn't need them. I was fortunate to have known you.

As long as Lake Mead is fresh in our minds, here's a short story about a freak accident my boss, Dion, had while on the lake.

One of the perks enjoyed by stagehands is the fact that they know showgirls. And if you happen to have a nice boat, well, some very fun and memorable times can be experienced on what is a very unremarkable lake. Showgirls and dancers don't like tan lines, and to avoid them they sunbathe nude. Now, stagehands spend many hours on the job convincing the girls that we're professionals, and that we've long since become used to seeing tits and asses, it's no big deal, so if you want to take all your clothes off and lounge around on deck, well, It's No Big Deal. My ass! Guys never change. Any chance to look at a young, hard body can't be squandered. Nothing like having a deck full of young, hard, naked female bodies… Hey, do you need me to put any oil on you?

Dion had a nice boat, all white. I believe it was twenty-three feet long (that's close, anyway), and if I'm not mistaken, the manufacturer's name was Howard. Because Dion kept the boat in excellent condition, he laid down the law regarding conduct and behavior while on his boat. The big rule that I remember was that you didn't get sand in the boat—or any kind of dirt, for that matter. See, Dion wouldn't say much if you broke the rules; you just didn't get another invitation.

On one of his outings, Dion and a couple of his pals put out to sea…okay, went out on the lake to drink some liquor, do a little illegal substance abuse, and enjoy a boating experience. For whatever reason   to get more gas or pick up a late straggler   they were heading for the dock when the freak accident happened.

As I understand it, when pulling into a dock, it's not unusual for the driver to stand up and steer the boat in, allowing for a better view and clearer perspective of the distance between boat and dock. Dion was four or five feet from the dock, standing up, when one of the passengers jumped off the bow onto the dock so as to keep the boat from rubbing up against it. Dion wasn't aware of this, and the sudden rocking motion caused him to lose his balance and fall against the side of the boat. He put his hand out to steady himself but his hand slipped. Now he was actually falling all the way out of the boat.

And he would have, if it weren't for the fact that his leg got tangled up in the steering wheel. Between the weight of his body going overboard and the angle of his leg tangled in the wheel something had to give, and it wasn't the steering wheel. It was Dion's leg, as close to a compound fracture as you can get.

As if that wasn't bad enough, his boat rode low in the water, and although most of his body went overboard, his trapped leg kept him from falling out completely. When his body came to a rest, his head was partially submerged under water.

He couldn't help but scream out in pain, which rewarded him with a mouth full of water. Now he was in serious danger of drowning if he didn't get immediate assistance.

I was always under the impression that Dion lived a charmed life; there just happened to be a couple of guys remaining on the boat who helped him out right away. You had to laugh, though, to hear Dion tell it, because when you first heard the story, no matter how he told it he came out looking like a drunken retard who couldn't keep his balance. And in the end you realized how lucky he was that he hadn't been alone.

Stan C. was usually a pretty nice fellow, although he had no problem asking a person to do a task which he considered unpleasant, for the simple reason that he felt such a task was beneath his stature. I was taught by my bosses that you should never ask a man on your crew to do any task that you yourself would not do. The other thing I was taught was that when you hold a position such as Department Head, or when you're in a position to delegate assignments, always be aware of how you treat the people under your direction; someday one of them might be your boss. And I can tell you it was good advice, because it's happened to me.

Stan, on the other hand, didn't much care what we thought; you did what he told you to do and furthermore, you did it his way, because that was the only correct way to do things. He would give his orders, then leave to do some pet project he was involved with at the moment, which had nothing to do with the job. As a matter of fact, it was usually framing pictures; he liked framing so much that he opened a framing shop. If the truth be told, the only true framing he did was that of framing to be a person with business experience, proven by the fact that his shop shut down three months after it opened.

Work calls at the Trop were very unstructured. Basically, you could take breaks whenever you felt the urge and no one really cared as long as the work was completed on time. Stan, however, made it a point to make it known just who the hell was in charge. He'd let you know when to take a break and he'd also let you know when it was over. The normal break is fifteen minutes, but Stan's breaks were thirteen and a half minutes. See, he factored in the time it would take to get from the break area back to the work area, and deducted that from the break time.

Stan's schedule was also nonnegotiable regarding the time a break could be taken during a work call. Two hours and fifteen minutes into the call—that was the only acceptable time. It didn't matter if it was a three-hour call or whatever; that's just the way it was.

It was an invitation to irritate Stan, and I recognized it immediately.

I knew Stan would come around to announce the break, so punctual you could set your watch by him. I would wait for him to come walking into the backstage area, and as soon as I knew he could hear me, I'd yell, "Break! Fifteen minutes, everybody. Break."

God, this would piss him off no end.

"Hey Phil, do you know what the worst problem with this crew is?"

Gee Stan, that's a tough one to answer; this isn't a trick question, is it? Wait a minute; something's coming to me. Wait—wait—I got it! The worst problem this crew has is that you're an idiot, and lazy. Well, lazy isn't bad; it's a quality I kind of admire. But where you're concerned, Stan, lazy makes me want to kick you right in the ass.

What I said was, "Tell me, Stan, please."

"There's too many chiefs and not enough Indians."

What's wrong, Stan, have to put up your own teepee?

"Gosh, Stan, so I guess this means you prefer to call "Break" from now on. I'm sorry, it's just that I thought a little help would be appreciated."

We, the crew, knew just how to push Stan's buttons. Shit, we spent enough time dreaming up ways to agitate him. Stan was lacking one major asset that we as individuals and collectively as a crew did possess: a sense of humor.

With Stan, every issue was serious. As the head of the Prop Department, it was his responsibility to maintain and repair all of the props used in the Folies show and, giving Stan his due, it was a pretty big job to handle. The Prop man has to be a jack of all trades: part carpenter, part electronic wizard, plastic and fiberglass repairman— you name it and a good Prop man has probably done it. Still, you've got to have a sense of humor.

After Stan's little talk about who the boss was and, therefore, who would "break" the crew from now on, it seemed only natural that if I could do something along the same lines, but step up the intensity a notch or two, then the crew might witness a part of Stan that they hadn't known existed. Maybe we'll call it a Nova Stan, because Stan was bald and when he stressed out, his face turned beet red; he did sort of resemble an unstable star.

Stan scheduled the next work call a week later, and as usual he gave us a list of things to do that couldn't possibly be completed in the six hours we were scheduled to work.

Stagehands never know what any given job might require them to do, especially when they put in shows for conventions. If someone has an idea, whether it is a conventional design or some wild futuristic set design, we can build it or put it together. Hell, I've helped build a couple of set pieces that were so strange that when we completed the project, we still had no clue as to what we had just built.

So even though Stan possessed the skills to perform his job in a professional manner, it was the simple things that baffled him. While we were working on "Mission: Impossible" Stan was in his little office, unpacking new picture easels to be assembled and used in his framing shop.

Passing by his office on my way to get a cup of coffee, I peeked into the Prop Room. Stan was standing there with a confused look on his face. What I assumed were the easel assembly directions were now just crumpled balls of paper lying next to the wastepaper basket.

"Don't you have enough to keep you busy?" he asked.

"I sure do; just getting some coffee. Hey, I think you dropped these." Picking up the mangled instructions, I lay them on his desk.

"Go. Go now. You are one big nuisance, you know that, Ronzone? A real pain in the ass."

"Bye." And off I went.

The time for our fifteen-minute break drew near and Stan showed up early to remind us that with his appearance he was the Chief, and he would "break" us at the proper time. He was glaring at me, almost daring me to open my mouth. He was disappointed.

Back to work after eleven minutes—you would almost believe that Stan was paying for our labor out of his own pocket.

Once again, I had to go by Stan's office because I needed a tape measure from the tool crib. This time, I heard him cussing.

"These goddamn things are missing screws. Piece of shit."

What I saw, partially assembled, looked nothing like the easel pictured on the box. It was too tall and sort of bent in a couple of places.

The tool crib was inside the carpenter's office. A narrow walkway separated the two offices. I took my time getting the tape measure; I was very quiet. Stan was beginning to get very upset and probably didn't realize I was next door.

"Fucker. You prick piece of shit."

Earlier, he had put one of the empty boxes beside the garbage can. Curious person that I am, I looked at the box for a moment. In the upper right corner was an "easy to assemble" label: "All you need is a Phillips screwdriver and a pair of pliers. Easy-to-read instructions. Goes together in minutes."

Yeah, well, Stan had been dicking around for almost two hours now. Not only that, but now there were hammering noises followed by the sound of a cordless screw gun. What the hell was he doing? Clearly, the label on the box made no mention of hammers or power tools of any sort. Stan was in trouble.

The crashing sound followed by a squeal of pain startled me a little.

"Oh, good goddamn, fucking mother sucker. Bastard. Ouch! Ouch! Fucker's on my finger."

It's funny how we talk to ourselves when there's a problem, things like, "You'd better fit, you son of a bitch," which could mean, "I'm just about finished putting this project together; I've got one more piece to attach and it better be the right size." Or it could mean, "How did that happen?" Which means, "Shit, I took the measurement and now a piece doesn't fit, you dumb bastard." And Stan was talking up a storm.

This had gone far enough; I couldn't, in good conscience, ignore a fellow stagehand who quite obviously needed assistance. Compassion for our brothers is what makes our bonds so strong, the willingness to help each other. Well, I wasn't going to let Stan down.

I entered the Prop office and what I saw was a man on one knee with a couple of his fingers caught in the part of the easel that folds together. Somehow the easel was stuck. Stan's fingers were a slight purplish color; when I got a little closer, I saw that blood blisters had developed, and it was these that were purple. The small beads of sweat dotting his forehead gave testament to the pain he was feeling.

I needed to act now: first thing, assist the injured party. Next, treat that party with understanding and compassion, regardless of how stupid a mistake they've made. As a paramedic, I'd been able to put appearances and personalities aside and focus on the medical problems and the ability to render relief in one form or another. Time to get it on.

"Wow, Stan, I could hear you scream all the way across the stage. Jesus Christ, that looks painful. What in God's name did you do? Hey guys, come and look at this!" So much for compassion; maybe I could make up for my rudeness by assisting in the extraction of his digits from the killer easel.

"Please hurry, my fingers hurt like hell." Stan was pleading, very much out of character if you ask me.

"Okay, okay, let's take a quick look and see what the damage is. Now stop jerking around and hold still."

I thought the situation called for a little humor, just to help Stan deal with the stress. "Okay, I know what the problem is, Stan; you've got your fingers pinned in that contraption and it's causing you immense pain."

"That's not even funny. Please help me."

I guess Stan thought that I was either really dumb for claiming to suddenly understand his situation when an infant could tell what was going on just by looking, or that I was incredibly insensitive, with a bad sense of humor. What he didn't know was that I was a couple of seconds away from freeing up his fingers.

Just as his temper was replacing his pain, he let his guard down; and just that quickly I knelt down, grabbed the easel, and pried apart the two pieces that held Stan captive.

"Oh, oh, what the fu—! Oh Christ, thank you, thank you, thank you so much. I was just about to cry, it hurt so bad. I mean, just look at these."

He held up his hand and it hurt me. What I saw was a hand with three regular fingers and two plump, purple sausages. Man, it was ugly.

Stan and I kind of bonded that day; he even gave the crew a longer break that afternoon.

A few minutes before it was time to clean up and go home, I was thinking about how Stan and I were now good buddies. And buddies often kid around and mess with each other, right? Right. So when I pulled my last little prank for the day, he couldn't get too mad; hell, I'd just saved his fingers.

Since I hadn't dared call "Break" that day, and since he was thinking about the pain he was in, he just wasn't thinking about me. I waited until he came out of his office and was just entering the backstage area when I yelled, "Wash up, guys, it's time to go home."

"God damn it, Ronzone, I can't fucking believe you. Retarded, yeah, that's it; you must be goddamn retarded. How am I supposed to be a boss and be a nice guy, too?" Stan was pissed.

"Well, you cou… I started to say.

"Shut up, don't say another goddamn word, do you understand me?"

I heard you and this time I'd better not push my luck, if I have any left. I'd better shut up.

"Well, answer me, goddamn it!"

Uh-oh. First of all, you told me to shut up and not say another word, now you want me to talk. I'm so confused; well, it's my own fault. "Yes, Stan, I understand, but…

"That's it! Go home, enough is enough. You can work on anybody else's crew, they're welcome to have you. I've lost all my hair; my blood pressure has gone right through the roof; now I have only one good hand. How am I supposed to do any framing now? No, don't answer that. I can't take any more. No more."

I never said I was the brightest guy. Now you can add, "good judgment." I hope this isn't the start of a long list entitled, "Things I never was."

Stan forgave me eventually and he even invited me to work on the prop crew again. Who said there's a sucker born every day? It's true, some guys just never learn.

Painting the concrete around the stage was a job that fell to the Prop Department. It took six guys, four to five hours, and thirty gallons of gray paint. It had to be done at night, and the following day had to be a dark day (no shows). That way, the paint had all day to dry.

But before the painting began there was lots of work to do. The first thing to be done was to move everything off the concrete onto the stage. Next, hot water and bleach were used to clean the concrete; this took a lot of mopping. The area to be painted was close to forty-five hundred square feet; every man had a twelve-inch roller and a bucket of paint. Oh yeah, before the rolling started, the whole perimeter of the backstage area had to be painted with a brush so that no roller marks would be seen on the walls. There were also many spike marks that required the use of a brush. It was a lot of work.

Stan had been talking to us a week before the painting call was scheduled to take place, acting as though this was a big deal, like his boss would be watching us very closely to make sure we didn't miss any spots. Then he made the mistake of voicing his concern for the state of our mental health, come painting night.

You see, for years the job was left to the Carpentry Department. I had been on the carpentry crew many times to do the painting call, probably half a dozen times prior to Stan's taking over, and this was actually his first time. Sometimes the spike marks, which were used to make sure that things were in their proper places while stored offstage, were mistakenly put in the wrong place. The spike marks themselves might be painted the wrong color. Since the Props Department determined what marks went where, it just made good sense to let them handle the job and make sure everything was done properly. That's why Stan was placed in the position of doing this job, as department head, for the first time.

In years past, the paint call was unique as far as work calls go. Because it was done so late, everyone except the painters had gone home. With the Main Curtain down and the rest of the stage locked up, the painters were isolated.

A tradition had started long ago whereby the head carpenter bought beer in, and as soon as the last patch of concrete was painted, the beers would be passed out. Of course as the years went by, the beers were opened earlier and earlier until you had your first beer just so you could get in the mood to paint. By the time we were ready to go home, everyone had drunk five or six beers.

It was finally paint night. The second show ended and we took a twenty minute break, changed into old clothes and, right before we clocked in, smoked a couple of joints, did a couple serious lines of coke, and just to put that extra twist on things, took a Lude.

First stop was the refrigerator to grab a brew, then a paintbrush and get to work. I'd just walked in the back door when one of the guys said, "Stan, there's no beer in here; where'd you put the beer?"

"I know how things were done around here before, but it's different now. You guys get all fucked up and the work doesn't get done. You guys nowadays don't know how to work. All you want to do is party. Well, not on my crew. Okay, okay, settle down before you pop a vein. Forget about the beer; let's just all get along."

So we started to paint, and it was a good two hours before we saw Stan again. It was a good thing, too, because I was just getting ready to call "break."

After the break, Stan picked up a paint bucket and roller and went over to a corner area and started to paint. We were shocked; he never worked with us. Maybe this was a bonding moment. Could he want to be just one of the guys?

"Hey Stan, it's nice to have you with us," one of the guys said.

"No, actually, I think you guys are going really slow, so I figured if I was out here, you guys would work faster."

So much for male bonding.

We had a long-running game we'd play while painting. We'd discreetly try to paint a guy into a space where he'd be trapped, surrounded by wet paint. It was really difficult to do anymore, because most of the crew had been trapped at one time or another, and unless you waited for the paint to dry, the other option was to walk through the wet paint, then have to clean up a big mess. Stan, however, had never painted before, so before he knew it, he was trapped.

The rest of the crew was on the deck laughing when Stan looked up and wondered what we were laughing at. Before we could say anything, Stan put his roller down and started to walk over to us.

I guess he never even saw the wet paint, because the second he stepped on it, his feet went out from underneath him and he fell flat on his back—like a guy who falls into a pool with all his clothes on and thinks, "If I can just move fast enough, I can get out and not be completely soaked". He moved quick as a cat, turned over on his hands and knees, and was starting to get up when his hands slipped out from underneath him. Stan went down again, on his stomach this time.

We were speechless; we were watching a drowning man, and it was funny. I knew we were going to pay hell for this, but it didn't matter. We couldn't have stopped laughing if you'd put a gun to our heads.

"Hey Stan, would you stop fooling around? Now I've got to paint it again," some smart-ass yelled.

Like I've said several times, I'm not the smartest guy around, so before I could stop myself, I blurted out, "Hey, it's the human paint roller."

Oddly enough, when Stan finally got to dry land he didn't even get mad. In fact, he even cracked a smile. "I hate you guys, you know that, but that had to look pretty funny, huh? Well, you know what, I'm gonna change and then I think I could use a beer. How about you guys?"

That was a spiritual moment for Stan. He seemed to lighten up after that. Even the next time we had the paint call, when someone drew the outline of a human form on the ground like they do with chalk at a murder crime scene, with Stan's name on it, Stan was the first to laugh about it. You gotta have a sense of humor.

CHAPTER 10

ROB'S ROACH CIRCUS AND PHANTOM PENIS EXHIBITION

Rob P. had many talents and farting was just one of them. Over the years he proved that idle minds are dangerous minds—mischievous, at the very least.

Rob always kept an eye open for cockroaches; I even think he spread food around so he had a chance to collect the biggest and strongest roaches the Trop had to offer. Usually, by the beginning of the show, he'd already collected quite a stable of those dirty little suckers.

"Hey, Phil, what do you think?" I would look over at Rob and he would be tying a piece of string around a particularly large roach. "Isn't she beautiful?"

"Oh yeah, Rob, looks like she's strong, too, comes from good breeding stock, I imagine."

"Yeah, I think so, too; well, we're gonna go for a little walk, see some of the girls. Want to come?"

"No, but you go on ahead; I kinda like to just sit back and listen for the screams."

But Rob gets bored easily, so it was just a matter of time before he found a new use for his roach collection.

The Can-Can Set is the trademark feature of our show. Downstage, closest to the audience, is where the tables are set up. On these tables are plastic champagne glasses and bottles, with the glasses turned upside down. There is also a bar unit with the same setups of bottles and glasses.

Rob's favorite thing to do with his little cockroach friends was to run out onstage during the Can-Can setup and put roaches under as many upside-down glasses as he could before the cast arrived onstage to do the number. He couldn't do this very often because the cast would expect it, so he just did it every once in a while to catch them off guard. Once we knew he'd placed the roaches, we'd peek through the curtain to see what would happen.

The showgirls would come and sit at the tables, and a few would stand at the bar unit as if waiting to be served a drink. The beautiful thing was the timing. The cast members, who had to change clothes and hurry to get to their places, didn't have time to really look around. The lights would go dark so that when the curtain was flown to reveal the Can-Can number, the lights could go up suddenly to add to the effect. As soon as the lights came back on, it was show time.

The tables were covered with tablecloths so the glasses didn't move easily, but the bar top, which was smooth and flat, was a hive of activity.

Roaches don't like light, so when it got bright all of a sudden they ran for cover, taking the glasses with them. Doing the same thing night after night, it was funny watching the girls reach for a glass that wasn't there, or one that was mysteriously moving across the bar top, seemingly under its own power.

Many times it wasn't until a girl had picked up her glass and raised it to her lips that she would see a big old roach scurrying around in her glass. These were the best—they'd let out a scream you could hear across the street. They would throw their glass down and run around, looking at their hands and arms for more roaches. Sometimes we'd see the roaches crawling around on the girls' dresses, and if one got lucky, it would go down the front of the dress. Wow, then you'd really see something special. We used to call it "the spazz dance." These poor girls, the first thing they'd do was start ripping their clothes off. Hats would go flying, blouses would be ripped open, and sometimes the skirt even came off. It was hilarious, but there was usually a price to pay, a reprimand of some sort. Rob took it like a man. He never implied that he had any accomplices, always just took the blame.

Some people enter the "Stagehand Hall of Fame" by means of a single spectacular act; others, by a continuous effort which spans their career as stagehands. Rob fits into this second category. So the final nominating action, of which Rob was the sole creator and distributor, was the "Phantom Peter."

I'll try in vain to recreate this masterpiece for you:

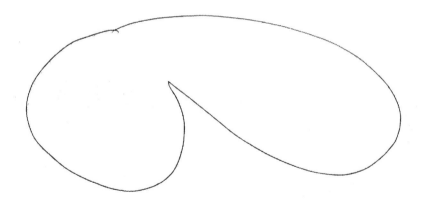

That's absolutely terrible, but you get the idea. This symbol graced not only the halls of the Tropicana, but also many other institutions.

These "Phantom Peters" started out innocently enough at six to eight inches long. Years later they were recorded as covering the back side of the shadow box piece, which measured well over nine feet long and two to three feet tall. They could appear any time, anywhere, and you just had to laugh.

Debbie, the wife of the Entertainment Director and Producer, was given the job of conducting backstage tours of the showroom during the day. It wasn't uncommon for us to be working during these tours, and I have happened to be standing close by when Debbie would come to the rail area with twenty or thirty tour guests. Now Debbie, who has been exposed to stagehands and their sense of humor for more years than she cares to admit, is not alarmed when someone in the tour says, "My God, young lady, what in Heaven's name is that drawing up there?"

Debbie answers, almost with pride, "Oh, that's just a 'Phantom Peter'; they're all over the place."

Well, for a Christian group from Georgia or Alabama, some place like that, a big nine-foot cock and balls is just something they don't see every day. Nor do they find the humor it was meant to create. So because of the number of complaints, the "Phantom Peters" were ordered to be eliminated—but they continued to appear from time to time. It was Rob's way of marking his territory.

CHAPTER 11

NOW YOU SEE HIM, NOW YOU DON'T

One of the practices that Dion, my boss, tried to instill in us was the idea that we knew what the guys to the left and right of us had to do, so if a guy missed a cue or was about to miss a cue, someone else might notice and be able to correct the situation before any damage was done.

During the show, there was a cue that the guy to my left had to do that was a little tricky, especially if you had never done it before. A box, what they call an "apple box" to be exact, was set down on the stage left side, twenty feet or so from the audience and maybe ten feet from the stage left masking.

At the start of the number a boy dancer was standing on the box, and in a swing that had been lowered sat a girl. The period was eighteenth century, so the girl wore an elegant ballroom gown, the boy a fancy long coat and stockings, complete with a white powdered wig.

The boy would push the girl on the swing, which took her a little ways over the audience at the farthest point of the swinging arc, then back to the boy, and he would push her out again. This happened three times. At the end of the third swing the boy would be looking out to the audience, not at the girl on the swing, with his arms spread wide open. He would then jump off the box, go to the front of the swing, help the girl down, and they'd go dancing off across the stage.

What the audience didn't know was that a stagehand offstage was actually controlling the motion of the swing. When the boy pushed the girl on the swing, a stagehand was pulling down on a rope until he reached a tape mark on the rope which told him that it was now time to let the rope slide back through his hands, until the swing was almost back down to the boy on the box. The stagehand would then clamp down on the rope until the swing actually stopped. The boy on the box would push the swing again and the whole process would be repeated two more times.

Even though I had seen it done many times, I'd never actually had to do it. I'd never had the chance to cover someone who wasn't there to do their cue; usually they were covering for me. I waited. Time for the cue was fast approaching, and still the guy who was supposed to work the swing was deeply involved in a card game.

Here was my big chance to cover someone else, just for once to show Dion I wasn't a fuck-off. Now, what I should have done was tell the guy that he was about to miss his cue, and in time for him to get there. What I did, though, was to step right up to the rope and wait for the cue to begin.

The boy was on the box. He pushed the swing. I took up the slack and pulled the girl out until I saw the tape on the rope. At that point I let the rope slide back through my gloves until it was almost back to the boy, and brought it to a complete stop. The boy pushed and we did the routine all over again. Easy as pie—plus, I get a hearty thanks from the guy who missed his cue. I was finally being that valued employee that Dion had the right to expect.

For some reason, on the third and final swing motion, instead of bringing the swing to a stop on its descending arc, I just let the rope go. No one was more surprised than me when that girl and her swing knocked the boy so far off the box that he actually landed off the stage. Well, maybe the boy was more surprised.

I just knocked the shit out of him. When he got his wind back, which was amazingly quick, he was up and staggering back out onto the stage. One shoe was missing, his shirt was in shreds, and his wig was hanging off to the side of his head. He was at center stage before be remembered that his dancing partner was still on the swing. The number was ruined, because he never caught back up to the music.

"Sorry Dion, I guess I need a little practice." So I practiced every evening between shows for forty-five minutes for the next two weeks. To the dancer I had to make a sincere apology, which he truly deserved.

CHAPTER 12

THAT'S NO BULL, THAT'S A PINATA

The Entertainment Department had a warehouse that was not on the Tropicana property. If I'm not mistaken its size was twenty thousand square feet, perhaps larger. "Warehouse" is not an adequate word. I think "graveyard" (excuse me if I lose my concentration here but my good friend and mentor, Mike, just farted, so things are a little hazy) would be a better description.

During the day it was a very ordinary place, kept for the most part as storage for scenery and props. Some items were used on a regular basis and others had been sitting for years. Part of the space we kept clear because we did quite a bit of building in those days. We worked long days over there and during the winter months, when the sun went down, that place became downright eerie. Maybe that's because when things were quiet, you noticed the little creaks and groans from pieces of shows that were now just a memory, almost as if they were crying out for one last curtain call.

A robot that once had moved on rollered feet with arms that swung, a head that turned, and eyes that lit up—a once jolly little machine— was now piled in a heap with his other broken-down brothers.

Bamboo huts, fencing, and a large stack of walls and roofs that when put together made a small western ghost town…The Hawaiian outrigger tipped up on its side, one paddle dangling, a chain holding it hostage…A giant Times Square arch with a huge clock perched high atop, its hands stopped at midnight…A couple of old wooden soldiers, the kind a young boy might have   only these were life size, with missing eyes, arms hanging at grotesque angles, and uniforms torn and dirty.

Lined up against one wall were jukeboxes, brightly colored but with dust making them look broken down and in need of repair. Against another wall was a stack of Central Park fence units, enough to go around a small park.

In back of the small office were more rooms filled with old costumes, shoes, wigs, and all sorts of strange apparel. Moth-eaten racks of long coats, velvet ballroom gowns and old capes, all a tribute to once glorious and elegant editions of the Folies Bergere, times when ambience was the first and most important consideration for presenting a show. Money was no concern.

And finally, the old equipment room. A giant carbon arc projector, and what were surely antique spotlights. Old lights that once held gels of many different colors, some probably twenty or thirty years old, now just piled one on top of another. Nests of old cable and stage plugs, their days of usefulness long since past.

If there weren't some old ghosts hanging around there, there aren't any ghosts. Anywhere.

But among all these things, none had a more celebrated life than the Bull.

This was no ordinary bull; he stood about twelve and a half feet tall at the tip of his horns when he was standing up. A man could almost walk under its stomach area without bending over. It was a good five feet wide and boasted a length of over twelve feet. He was a massive fellow.

The Bull had a certain mystique, and so it came as no surprise that his presence was requested for many different events. However, the Bull was not an easy guest to accommodate. For instance, just arranging transportation for the big fellow was no small matter. The hotel's flatbed truck seemed to be the only answer. It took an army to carry the big stud: one man on each leg if you had enough guys; one under the stomach area; then you had to have one guy lead the way, clear a path, so to speak.

And it was funny, because when we carried the Bull through the casino, or out by the pool area—in fact, just about anywhere—the guy clearing the way usually had his hands full. When people saw the Bull coming, they would just naturally be drawn closer until there was a small crowd everywhere he went. People would come up and just stop right in front of the Bull, not even paying attention to the struggling men whose job it was to move the beast safely.

A man might get injured if he wasn't careful. One time while the Bull was en route to a party, one of the guys holding a front leg stumbled and fell down; then the other guy in front let go, unable to carry the weight. There were skinned knees, sore backs, and a lot of swearing. Another time at the warehouse, the Bull was hanging up in his spot about ten feet off the ground. We were getting ready to get the big guy, and one of the crew was just undoing a knotted rope to lower the Bull when the rope slipped through his hands. The Bull came crashing down, landing on its four legs. Luckily Jim, a part time worker backstage, was a short fellow. Even though he was standing up, his five-foot, five and a half inch body had plenty of room to spare when the Bull fell. Jimmy, however, was a cowboy, and as cowboys like to wear cowboy hats, Jimmy had his hat on and it didn't fare so well. When I heard, "Oh, Jesus Christ, my fucking hat just finished its last rodeo, folks," I looked over and there was Jimmy, with his hat brim down around his neck and the rest smashed down around his face. He looked pretty damn ridiculous. All he was missing was a pair of six shooters hanging around his knees.

If that old Bull could talk, he'd tell you a few stories. One story would be how in a rush he was forced into an elevator and, instead of getting off the next floor up as planned, some joker pushed the sixteenth floor button. Once we passed our floor, we were going up to the sixteenth floor whether we wanted to or not. It turned out to be quite entertaining. When the doors opened onto the fifth floor a Japanese couple were somewhat startled; they went jabbering away back down the hall.

The C.E.O. and several Vice Presidents at the Trop found the Bull useful, each for a different reason. One person of Spanish descent thought it would be a great ornament at his dinner party; another actually asked us if it could hold candy and small presents. Well yeah, except who's the bad little son of a bitch who's going to hit this Bull? And when it breaks open, which kid will get hurt when a hundred pounds of candy comes falling out?

One day a terrible thing happened. The Bull was requested to appear at a party. Unfortunately, this time the old Bull was too big to get into the room. Well, we decided, guess we'll load the Bull back on the truck and take him home.

The Vice President, who wouldn't be V.P. if he weren't used to making difficult decisions, said, "Cut it in half." Whoa, whoa, wait a minute, you didn't just say, "Cut it in half," did you? You just can't cut Ferdinand in half; that's just not right.

Bottom line, we now had two parts to the Bull. No more climbing on his back, no more struggling with the beast. The Bull never quite recovered from the radical surgery we performed that day. It's like he never quite fit together, never looked quite right. Also, when we moved him, I always seemed to get stuck carrying the back half. It was kind of embarr-ass-ing (get it?) walking among the public, two guys each holding a leg with a big ass between us. Well, once you got used to the laughter, the worst was over.

Two or three years passed and one day the Bull had vanished. It had been cut up and put in a large dumpster. All that could be seen were those big yellow horns sticking up a little. It was a sad, sad day.

CHAPTER 13

A ROUGH NIGHT IN JAIL

The entertainment industry is difficult to describe when referring to the people who work within its parameters. I cannot think of any other industry containing such diversification, where people are interacting with each other to achieve a common goal.

In my experience over the last twenty-seven years, there is one simple concept that is vital to a long and happy partnership with this industry: a lack of prejudice, in any shape or form. And the people who are not able to operate by this simple principle experience little if any enjoyment, or worse, are exiled from this business in one fashion or another.

Working a production show, I was exposed to the gay element, up close and personal. My parents taught me at a young age to respect all people without exception. Of course, they also taught me that respect is a two way street, and I had the right to expect it in return. It's how I think friendships should work also, but I've been disappointed more than once in that area.

Anyway, for many years, I had the pleasure of working with a fellow known as Pat. He was a talented dancer, had a great sense of humor, and would give you the shirt off his back if you needed it. Pat was also as gay as they come.

One year to celebrate his birthday the other cast members threw him a giant surprise party after the second show. Because Pat was a popular person, he received a mountain of gifts. The alcohol and other party favors were flowing freely. The party turned into a wild bash and at some point moved down onto the stage. One of the sound technicians piped in music through the house sound system. Not to be outdone, the head electrician created some lighting effects, complete with mirrored balls. Even the rail contributed by lowering a backdrop, and all of a sudden the stage had been transformed into our own private disco.

As the party progressed, inhibitions broke down and things got crazy. Shirts, blouses, shoes, socks—soon the stage was littered with clothing. Naked bodies were swaying to the music. Others were just relaxing, cast and crew mingling, everybody having a great time.

Sometime during those early morning hours, one of Pat's birthday gifts was passed around the stage: a life size blow-up doll. Only this wasn't a female doll; it was a male doll. Someone had taken the time to blow it up and when it was completely inflated, it put us normal guys to shame. But it still had those funky lips that formed that shocked, surprised look—you know, the O-shaped mouth.

As it happens, the doll was designated to be a special memento dedicated to this evening. Accompanying the doll was a felt pen, so that anyone who wanted to record a special message to Pat could do so on the doll. It's no surprise that its eleven-inch cock was entirely covered; in fact, by the time the doll had made its way around the room, very little area remained unsigned.

With the horizon showing the first signs of a rising sun, the party finally came to an end. Pat, who had gotten completely wrecked hours ago, brought his Volkswagen Beetle up to the gate leading to the backstage area. There, with the help of his friends, he loaded all his gifts into his car and was just about to drive away when someone came running frantically up to his window and told Pat to wait a second—he'd forgotten his doll. When the doll arrived, Pat decided that it would take too much time to deflate his doll. So he opened up the sunroof. After the doll was unceremoniously shoved into the car, a good portion of the body and head were sticking up through the roof.

Henderson, Nevada, just minutes away from Las Vegas, was

where Pat resided. Henderson's roots date back quite some time and I guess you could best describe its character as "shit-kicking redneck." The small police department had a no-nonsense reputation, which pretty well described its small police station and jail.

Pat was cruising down the road just minutes from home when he committed a minor traffic violation. Aside from that, I'll bet the police officer was curious who the clown was, driving down the road with a blow-up porn doll sticking out the roof of his car. I'm sure Pat rattled off a few of his funniest one-liners, which the cop thought were not funny (more likely, offensive). Anyway, he was interviewed and then asked to take a sobriety field test, which he promptly failed.

Can you imagine some of the questions the officer might have asked Pat that morning?

Pat: "What did I do, Officer? I wasn't speeding."

Cop: "I pulled you over, son, because I couldn't help noticing your funny-looking friend's head sticking out the roof, or that large dick obstructing your vision."

Pat: "Oh, that's not so big, Officer, I could still see."

Cop: "Where are you headed, boy?"

Pat: "Just going home, sir, I live just around the corner."

Cop: "Have you been drinking last night? When was your last drink, boy?"

Pat: "No sir, I did not have one drink last night."

Cop: "Okay son, I need you to blow into this breath-a—no, no, goddamn it, I didn't say blow me, I said blow into this tube, boy. Damn queer."

Pat: "Christ, my mistake. Okay, all right, I understand now. Ready?"

Cop: "Blow, goddamn it, sonny, I'm not fooling around here."

Pat: "Phatttt..."

Cop: "I'm going to place you in my car while I have a little chat with your buddy." Cop places Pat in patrol car, goes to interrogate passenger. "Okay partner, can I see some identification please?"

Doll: "........

Cop: "Where you guys headed?"

Doll: "........

Cop: "Are you trying to be a wise guy? We don't appreciate that around here, son." All of a sudden the cop grabs the doll, yanks it out of the car and wrestles it to the ground, finally putting the handcuffs on. "You all think you're tough guys, don't you? Well, you and your friend are both going to the pokey. Now you want to say something, bud? Hey, don't look so surprised."

Doll: "Ptsssss…

Cop: "You don't look so big now; in fact, I better make those cuffs a little tighter. They look like they're about to fall off."

Cop talks to Pat and Friend on way to station:

Cop: "Yeah, I've been a cop for a while. You're name's Pat, right? Right. Well, like I was saying, I been a cop for a while, Pat, and I got this sixth sense, you could say. Now you're probably a pretty decent fellow, but your friend's a real slime ball. Yeah, I know when they're hiding something. Yeah, you can tell just by looking at him. Every time I ask him a question, he just looks surprised as hell."

Pat: "Yes, sir."

Cop: "I'll tell you another thing. He's done a lot of time, judging from the ink on that sucker's body."

Pat: "I don't know, sir, we just met yesterday."

Cop: "Oh, by the way, you failed the breath test badly. When I asked if you drank last night you shouldn't have lied to me, son."

Pat: "I didn't lie, Officer, I wasn't drinking last night, sir. I started drinking about two this morning and that's the truth."

Cop: "When we get to the station you'll be booked, but your friend here doesn't look so good. May have to take him to the E.R. first."

By now, Pat's having a pretty bad time; he's coming down now and he's tired, got a headache, feels like he might even throw up. He's been locked up in the drunk tank with several other guys who look real bad-ass to Pat; he's sure they're bikers. Now they're looking at Pat; they know they don't like him but they just can't figure out why. Pat's depressed now; his birthday's ruined, sitting in the slammer, feeling like shit. It can't get any worse than this. It just can't.

Wanna bet?

The cop appears at the door and Pat looks like a person who's just caught a glimpse of the Grim Reaper. And the cop's not alone. The door opens and in flies Pat's new friend, his personally signed blow-up doll.

"Didn't want you to get feeling all alone in there, so I brought you your buddy; hey, you can thank me later."

As the door slams shut, Pat looks at his cellmates. They're all smiling now, and the last thing Pat said he heard was the biggest one saying, "Oh yeah, come to Papa, sugar puss." He thinks he threw up after that. Happy birthday, Pat.

CHAPTER 14

IT'S GOD—NO, IT'S THE DRUNKEN CUE CALLER

Before they built the Tiffany Room, which is our present showroom, there was the old showroom. Its name escapes me at the moment, but during its day it was pretty impressive. However, compared to the new showroom, it was very small. Very intimate, its seating capacity was about four hundred and fifty people, not a bad seat in the house. It was really very nice.

The day we were told that the old theater was to be torn down, well, it saddened us all. For a while though, it became a place where smaller production shows and musicals were booked.

A popular musical show, came in one day. It was to run for two weeks and if it drew good crowds, the show was to be extended. The cast had been working together from the beginning; there were only two other people who traveled with the show. One was the lighting director, who had just been recently hired; the other was part Head Carpenter and part cue caller for the show.

Ernie was a vital person with regard to a smooth-running show. In fact, with a new crew working the show whenever it opened in a different city, if Ernie wasn't present there wouldn't be a show, at least not for a day or two. As cue caller, he basically told everyone what to do and when.

As Head Flyman for the show I was particularly reliant on Ernie, for the simple fact that without his direction I didn't know when to open the main curtain, when to take out or bring in scenery or backdrops; it all depended on Ernie's commands.

There was one other thing that Ernie was good at: drinking. God, that man could drink. We didn't know this until the show had been up and running for a couple of days.

In those days, many stages had a small area built to one side of a stage, elevated some fifteen to twenty feet, called the "crow's nest". Here the cue caller could oversee the stage, call cues, and keep an eye on the show. The "crow's nest" in our room was ten feet below the rail deck. (In this showroom, the rail was elevated off the stage floor about thirty feet. It served as both rail and loading bridge. In the new theater, the rail is located at stage level and the loading bridge is sixty feet above the rail. The loading bridge is where we add or take off weight to counterbalance the set pieces.) So this meant that when I was working the rail, I could lean over the safety railing and peek right down into the "crow's nest".

Getting back to the show, we ran smoothly for the first couple of days. Then Ernie must have felt the crew was competent, so he started to have himself a little nip or two during the shows.

About the fourth day of the show's run, toward the end of the first show it was becoming difficult to hear and understand Ernie. By the second show it was a real challenge. No one on the house crew much cared, because hell, we were having a drink too, so we were all sort of on the same wave length. However, the electrical crew also shared the intercom system we used, and the L.D. (Lighting Director) could hear Ernie talking. He passed the information on to the Producer, who flew into town the following night to confront Ernie.

But we didn't know this, and as it turned out it was one of the biggest mistakes the Producer ever made. Not because he came down to check things out, but because of the way he conducted his spy operation and the subsequent bust.

The next evening we were being monitored. I was safe because I made it a point never to talk on the headsets unless I had a specific question. The first show ended. Nothing happened. We were still unaware of anything unusual.

The second show started and Ernie was hammered. Twenty minutes into the show, after a particularly hard cue for Ernie to say in his condition, an unfamiliar voice broke over the air:

"Ernie, this is Paul E. Something, you know, the Producer. Are you okay?"

Ernie: "Paul, Paul, how the hell are you doing, buddy? It's great to talk to you. Where the hell are you calling from, you old son of a bitch?" (I guess Ernie forgot he was on the headset, not a phone.)

Paul: "I'm fine, Ernie. Ah…I'm not on the phone, Im talking to you over the headset.

Ernie: "Oh, the hell you say. Hey, how's that faggot partner of yours? Uh, where you calling from again? Oh, just a second, I got to call some cues." (Paul let him do the cue calling.)

Paul: "Ernie, listen, I'm in the light booth and there's sort of a problem. Have you been drinking at all?" (Now Ernie had a caution sign go off in his head.)

Ernie: "Where did you say you were? What did you just say, Paul? Where the hell are you, anyway?"

Paul: "I said I'm in the light booth and it sounds to me like you've been drinking, Ernie."

Ernie: "You in the light booth? What's going on here? How come you're in the light booth? Couldn't you afford a ticket, ya fuck?"

Paul: "I need to talk to you after the show Ernie; we need to settle some things."

Ernie: "What things? Are you fucking spying on me or something? Oh shit, now you made me miss calling a fucking cue, you fucker."

Paul: "Don't talk to me like that, Ernie. You're getting yourself in deeper trouble, pal."

Ernie: "I'm not your fucking pal. In fact I never did like you or your funny little friend, the fuck, I'm doing just fine. You got a problem, Paul?"

Paul: "I'll see you after the show. You'd better make other plans; I don't think you're going to work out."

At this point I looked down into the "crow's nest" and saw Ernie sit back in his chair. I thought he was laughing.

Ernie: "You can't fire me. You got a problem?"

Paul: "Ernie you little shit, if I could I'd fire you right now, you little bastard."

Ernie: "Know what, you got a problem. Oh shit, now I just missed calling more cues. Fuck, stop talking to me; you're making me fuck up. Oh yeah, I was saying YOU GOT A PROBLEM, Paul, right now, 'cause I just quit. You're so smart and high and mighty, you call the show. I'm not talking any more."

At that point several things were about to happen, none of them good. And I realized something just then that I remembered the rest of my life. Never rely on anyone to tell you what to do any longer than you have to. Learn the show as fast as possible, especially if you're head of a department.

The whole conversation up to this point was taking place during one of the longer numbers in the show, and it was now coming to an end. No one knew what to do and we all thought we just heard that the only guy who could tell us had just quit. Just to confirm that, I looked over the rail down into the nest and Ernie was kicked back in his chair, feet up, with his headset resting in his hands.

"Ernie!" I yelled. "What do I do? What do I bring in, preset, what the fuck do I do?"

No answer.

Meanwhile, Paul's just understood the mega-mistake he's made. Even as Producer he doesn't know every cue of this show, not even close. This is one of five shows he's got going on; that's why he's hired guys like Ernie to run the show for him.

Paul: "Ah...Ernie, Ernie are you there? Ah...Ernie, come on, answer me. Come on Ernie, talk to me babe, this isn't funny. Ernie, answer me god damn it! I mean Ernie, let's talk about this, huh? How about it?"

I needed to make a decision; the number was ending and something had to come in so the scene could change. Was it the main, the chiffon, the black traveler? What was it? Okay, I'll bring in the traveler. The number ended. Black traveler in. WRONG. BIG WRONG. Shit, it's too far upstage; things need to happen behind the chiffon, which is ten feet further downstage. It's messed up, I'm completely lost. Just then Ernie put his headset back on.

Paul: "Ernie, you can't do this to me, Ernie. Goddamn you, you little fuck, do you hear me?"

Ernie: "Yes."

Paul: "Yes, what? What the fuck are you doing?"

Ernie: "Knock, knock."

Paul: "What? What did you say?"

Ernie: "Knock, knock."

It's amazing what one person can get another person to do when they've really put the screws to them.

Paul: "Knock, knock? What do you mean, 'knock, knock'?"

Ernie: "Knock, knock. You're supposed to say, 'Who's there?'"

Paul: "God damn it Ernie, you have no idea what you're doing. Think about later. This is going to follow you forever."

Ernie: "Say it. Say, 'Who's there?'"

Paul: "I'm not going to say, 'Who's there'."

Ernie: "Ha, you just said it. Who's there? I'll tell you. Not me! 'Bye."

And with that, we never saw Ernie again. That night the show stopped, unable to continue without Ernie. The main came down, the audience was given their money back and free passes to the next performance the following evening. The reason given for the shutdown? An injury to one of the principals (actors).

The next day we were called in to work at 7:30 in the morning and were introduced to Ernie's replacement. Rehearsals ran all day long, right up until show time. The show must go on.

CHAPTER 15

AND THE LUCKY WINNER IS...

When you think of Las Vegas, one of the images that comes to mind is luck. Lady Luck, as they say here. Now, I don't know where all these lucky people are or where they went, but they're sure not around me. The only thing I ever won was when I was eight years old. My grandmother took me to a church ice cream social. We were given tickets for a drawing that was to be held right before the social ended.

As time drew nearer to the drawing, I could hardly contain my excitement. I guess that, being a small kid among all those adults that evening, the excitement of a drawing was about all there was to look forward to.

It was time. I pulled my ticket from my pocket for the hundredth time. By now it was all crumpled up and the numbers were barely legible. As the gentleman stepped up to the microphone to announce the winning numbers, I broke out in a cold sweat. Five numbers; who was I kidding? Even though at that age I didn't understand much about percentages and odds, I still understood that a lot of people had tickets and that to win I'd have to be lucky.

Three drawings: two consolation prizes, one main prize. The main prize had to be good, I knew it just had to be. With the first two drawings completed, I was feeling kind of disappointed. Only one chance left, but still the main prize was up for grabs. The first two numbers matched, but the third didn't. Oh well, it was time to find my grandmother so we could go home. Wait a minute. The man was back at the microphone. For whatever reason, they needed to pick another number.

This time he read them off real fast, as if he was in a hurry to go. I looked at my ticket and tried to repeat the numbers in my head. Oh God, I think they match. I'm sure they match. Almost as if he read my mind, he repeated the numbers.

"I got 'em, I got the numbers, I won!" This I yelled as I ran up the aisle toward the man who held my prize.

Oh, this was great. I knew this was going to be a great prize and my imagination ran rampant. Maybe money—it could be a fortune, could even be a hundred dollars. Didn't I hear someone mention that earlier? Oh God, I can't even imagine, this is gonna be so good.

Finally I was there next to the man. He reached out to shake my hand and offered his congratulations. Come on, come on, let me have it. I want my prize. I've waited long enough. The man handed me a small box wrapped in gift paper. I was a little disappointed. No money? Who were those liars? Oh well, this box, even though it was sort of small, was heavy and that was a good sign, right?

After snatching it out of his hand, I ran to a nearby table. There I sat and began to tear off the wrapping paper. I had no idea what it could be, but those last couple of seconds my little heart felt like it was going to burst. A white box, no indication of what could be inside. Just a second more and my prize would no longer be a mystery.

Success! It's a shiny…it's a…no, no, wait a minute. It's a…it's a…it's a big, cheap, good for nothing combination lock. Crap, what a letdown. What the hell does a boy my age want with this? So I traded it with one of the other winners for an ice cream scoop or some damn thing.

Twenty years later a weekly contest, or drawing, so to speak, was started backstage. Actually, it was the brainstorm of a fellow who ran the light board upstairs in the show.

This man, who was and still is a talented electrician and cameraman, decided that things needed to be livened up a bit, and he had just the thing to do that. He figured that we would hold a raffle. The cost was five dollars per ticket. He needed to sell at least ten tickets; if that happened, he then had enough money to pay for the prize. Fifty dollars was the going price for a blow job back then, and I guess he knew a couple of different hookers who were willing to do the job.

Thank God, for reasons I won't go into, the guys on the rail were pretty much excluded from this raffle, simply because the winner received his prize at a specific time during the second show. It was a time when we couldn't make it up to the light booth due to our cues.

Anyway, it became quite the popular activity. Guys would cash their paychecks between shows, then purchase their tickets. The average was two or three tickets per man. It's amazing that this raffle went on as long as it did. There was a clamor and some allegations of the raffle being fixed, since a few guys sure won quite often, and a couple of others never won. The girls who offered their services were also a little upset because they figured out that the number of tickets sold produced a surplus of funds over what they were receiving for their product. They wanted a raise.

Now every once in a while, if one of the line captains for the dancers, or the lead showgirl, would want to show a trainee some part of the show, they would take them up to the light booth where they could sit on a couch and look at the show through the large plate glass windows.

Finally came doomsday. He had won the raffle. This was a lucky guy, and he decided that the girl should do her thing while he's working the light board. He made one huge mistake, which would almost cost him his job. He relied on a fellow crew member to lock the door to the light booth after the "headhunter" came in.

Of all the people who could have come that evening, it was Debbie. She was the lead showgirl and the wife of the producer of the Folies, Larry. Debbie, who was one of the nicest and coolest girls around, had brought a new girl, who was auditioning for the show, into the light booth to watch a portion of the show that she was in the process of learning. I guess even Debbie, who I'm sure wasn't pleased at all at the sight that greeted them, couldn't smooth over or ignore this situation because the new girl was freaking out. Debbie, being a good judge of character, knew this gal wouldn't keep quiet.

They had come in quietly so as not to disturb the guys working. He never heard them until the "headhunter" said, "Wow, you didn't tell me about this voyeurism shit, honey, that's gonna cost more."

This man, who was sort of caught up in the moment, didn't open his eyes right away, at least not until he recognized Debbie's voice screaming his name.

It doesn't get much worse than a guy reclining back in his chair, pants and underwear down around his ankles, and a girl kneeling between his legs naked, giving him the B.J. of his life. Then, an instant later, the big boss' wife is looking down with a complete stranger, and that good feeling deserts him. Big time.

The lucky winner got a call to meet Larry directly after the show. The next time I saw him was two weeks later; he was looking a little shy.

"Hey you big winner," I said. "Or should I address you as Mr. Lucky?"

"Shut up, will ya?" he answered. Another inductee into the "Stagehand Hall of Fame".

CHAPTER 16

ROCK-A-BYE-BABY

I mentioned Jack earlier in this story, a hard-working man, there's no question about it. The same man whose car was demolished by Trojan the horse.

Jack is a man of many hats; skilled at all levels of construction, he is in demand all year round. He also held a position on the rail. The only problem was that, many times during the show, Jack would be sleeping. We all knew he was working extremely hard; nevertheless, it was becoming a pain in the ass to have to make sure Jack was awake for every cue. Lots of times we'd let him sleep, just cover for him and do his cues ourselves.

It got so bad that one time on his way into work, a crew member saw Jack sleeping behind the wheel of his parked car. Jack left a day job and he arrived a half hour early and decided to take a little nap before the first show. The crew member decided he'd better wake Jack up because it was almost time to sign in, so he walked over to Jack's car and knocked on the window.

Jack woke up, saw who it was, and waved. The crew member turned and continued to walk into the hotel. All of a sudden he heard Jack's car start up and drive out of the parking lot. Jack told us later that he thought he fell asleep after the second show, so when the guy woke him up, he just started his car up and went home.

We were all getting tired of covering for him. Then one night Jack made a boo-boo. Somehow, a table was left by the rail, a small conference table six feet long and two feet wide, and Jack immediately recognized its possibilities: this table was made to sleep on.

Come the middle of the second show, the "Jack Alert" was in full effect. We covered for him for the better part of the show, but now came a set of cues that required all of us. Somebody yelled at Jack and that didn't work, so the guy went over and shook him a little. Still he didn't wake up.

Somehow we covered the cue, and we'd just about had it with him, so we all marched back there to give him a piece of our minds. But when we got back there, he looked so peaceful that we didn't want to wake him.

"Look," one of the guys said. "He looks like a dead guy on a table at the morgue; even his arms are crossed." Flowers appeared (stolen, actually, from a gazebo piece) and were placed ceremoniously on his chest.

"Wait, one of the acros has a camera. Let's get a picture." A few minutes later, snapshots were taken and we were getting kind of bored.

"Let's just cover him up with a sheet; that will look pretty funny and if he wakes up, he won't know where in the hell he is," someone offered. Covered in a sheet with more flowers piled on top of Jack, it did indeed look like a funeral.

Fifteen minutes before the show ended, someone came up with a rope and told us that there just happened to be a pulley rigged up a few feet over. Jack hadn't woken up through all this, so let's tie him down to the table, then fly the table out say, fifteen feet or so, and see what happens.

And that's just what we did. The show finally ended. We put everything away and headed for the door.

"Wait a minute," someone said. "We'd better go get Jack down. It's time to go home." We all looked at each other and a collective "Naa-a-ah" went up in unison.

The Security Department checks the backstage area twice a night; the first check is at 4:00 a.m., the second around 8:00 a.m. That night they were training a new employee so two security people were making the rounds. I knew Mike, one of the security people, and here's what he told me:

"We'd just opened the door at the entrance to the showroom, and even that far from the stage we heard what sounded like a muffled screaming or yelling. It was kind of eerie because the backstage area was completely dark. Since the sounds were unusual, we proceeded with caution.

"We walked along the side of the showroom until we entered the stage via the stairs. I then turned on the switch that illuminates the backstage area. At this point we established that we were hearing a person yelling, a very angry person; however, we were still unable to locate its origin. We checked the back area of the stage, and when we arrived at the rail area we found the person. I'd never seen anything like this before, so I called in my supervisor for assistance.

"It appeared that a male subject had been detained against his will by an as yet to be determined apparatus, which was swinging back and forth at a height of fifteen to twenty feet off the ground."

By now Jack had been airborne for about three and a half hours. God only knows when he woke up. He told us later that he had absolutely no clue where he was, the time, nothing—for a while, he was clueless. "Shit, you fucks, you know how I am, when you guys do wake me up, I don't know where I am half the time as it is. Now imagine waking up and you can't move because you're tied down, and on top of that I can't see nothing, I mean it's pitch black and if all that ain't bad enough, it takes me a second but I finally figure out that I'm swinging. I had absolutely no goddamn idea what the hell was going on. So I started yelling."

Mike, the security guard, confirmed this. "Oh yeah, he was yelling all right, and he was pissed. When we walked up, he knew someone was there. 'God damn it, somebody answer me, you fucks. Come on, I know you're there, fuckers. When I get down from here there's gonna be some sorry fuckers around here.'"

Mike told him, "Uh, sir, we're Tropicana security. You're backstage. Now just settle down; we'll have you down in just a minute. We're working on it now."

Unfortunately, Mike and the new guy weren't used to ropes and probably underestimated the weight, because when they were lowering Jack to the ground, the rope somehow got away from them and Jack and his makeshift table bed free-fell for the last five or six feet, crashing to the deck.

"Man, that guy was hot enough, you could have fried an egg on his forehead," Mike told me. "He said he's got a good, long memory and that there would be hell to pay. You guys were lower than dog shit. That was no way to treat an old timer in this business; fucking terrible."

By the time we saw Jack again, he was cooled off; in fact, even he had to admit it was pretty funny. On top of that, he didn't fall asleep at work for at least a week or so. I guess it was a lesson he just didn't want to learn. It was easier to wake him up than mess with him again.

CHAPTER 17

ACCUSED OF MURDER

Aside from working on the rail, I also served as Head Carpenter on most events that took place off the stage, mainly in the convention areas and in our pavilion.

The Tropicana sponsors a large New Year's party for their VIPs, and it's their largest party of the year. It takes weeks of preparation and about three days to install. It's a fairly large workforce and I've always considered it a challenge, but also a lot of fun.

I usually give the crew a small break after two and a half to three hours into the shift. We get coffee, bullshit a little, hit the restroom if we need to. So, as it happens, at break time one morning I had to go to the bathroom. Now I've touched on some of the farts that I used to let loose, and quite frankly, they were pretty bad, if I do say so myself.

This particular day I'd drunk my share of coffee, which tends to make me have a pretty healthy bowel movement later in the day. I entered the restroom and scurried over to the closest open stall that I could find. The first one was occupied so I slipped into the one right next to it.

I barely got seated and my bowels opened up; I admit it was pretty stinky. After that initial burst I was able to sit there and relax because the urgency of the moment had passed. So there I was, sitting there, when I noticed for the first time that the man in the stall next to me was saying something I couldn't understand. Not only that, but he was groaning quite a bit.

I like to crap in peace, I guess, because even though I felt kind of sorry for him, I just wished he'd shut up. I was thinking, "You know, if it's because he drank too much last night, well, shame on him. Now if it's something he ate, well I feel bad for the guy but either way, it's still the same to me. Just shut up and let me crap in peace."

Then the most extraordinary thing happened. I heard a groan that sounded different, then a bowel movement. All of a sudden I realized, from my past medical experience, that I was terribly mistaken with regard to what was taking place in the stall next to me. This guy wasn't suffering from too much to drink or from bad food; he was in the process of a heart attack.

As if to confirm this thought, a second later he tumbled off the commode and slipped under the stall wall. When he came to rest, the upper half of his body was now in my stall.

Hello, and by the way I was in kind of a strange position here, because I was still sitting on the crapper with a guy's head now resting on one of my shoes.

There have been a few times in my career as a medical responder that were just so uninspiring it's hard for me even to retell the story because it almost makes me physically toss my cookies. I'll give you an example. About the third month that I was working as an attendant for an ambulance company here in town, we went on a call which required my partner and me to give C.P.R. to a stricken individual. Back then it was true mouth-to-mouth, no bag. So there we were doing C.P.R., and to tell you the truth I was feeling pretty good about myself; I was actually breathing the life into another person. God, how wonderful is that?

After ten minutes or so I was getting a little tired, starting to feel like I might need some help. Anyway, my partner and I were about ready to switch places. As I took each breath my mouth was just an inch or so away from the victim's mouth. I was taking deep breaths because I had been breathing for both of us. Just as I was drawing in a big breath, Joe Victim suddenly choked and blew some big chunks, blowing a stream of vomit right into my mouth. Because

I was inhaling, I swallowed a good portion before I even knew what had happened.

And now here I was in the bathroom with my pants down, sitting on the john with an unconscious guy looking up at me. Why me? You know, I just wanted to crap in peace. No way.

I wiped real fast, pulled my pants up, and while I was doing this I was talking to the guy. "Hey, buddy, can you hear me? Can you hear me, guy?"

No response. I reached down and pinched the inside of his arm where it's real sensitive. No response.

Well, this was not good. I yelled, "Is anybody in here? I need some help; go get help." No answer. The guy's color was bad; I needed to get some air into his lungs, get his heart pumping. His stall was locked so I ended up pulling him all the way into mine, then out into the walkway. Now I had to perform one-man C.P.R. on a guy with his pants down and a trail of his poop behind because I had to drag him.

I was thinking, "God, if somebody comes in, they're gonna think I'm either robbing this guy or we're involved in some weird sex act, but that's okay, please God, just send somebody in here."

As God does, He gives us what we need. And so, a minute later, another fellow walked in.

"Help, please," I said between breaths. "Go get help; phone outside of bathroom. Call Security."

The Security team at the Tropicana deserves a round of praise for their quick response. It seemed like only seconds had passed when they arrived. Two of them took over for me and asked me to wait for them. I knew before I saw them that the fellow didn't make it; in fact, I was pretty sure he was dead before he hit the floor, but since I also knew that I wasn't qualified to make that final determination, I had to try to save his life.

After I wrote a statement out for Security, they released me to go back to work. Two days later, Security contacted me at home and said the family was in town to pick up the father's remains, and would I be so gracious as to meet with them for a few minutes? I told Security that I'd be happy to meet with them, and to ask them if there was anything that I could do.

It was already an awkward situation, compounded by the very nature of the location where this event took place. The family was interested in two things: number one, did he suffer? Number two, did the hotel respond quickly and was everything done that could be done at that time?

I went to Security later that day and they escorted me to the family's room and soon I was sitting in a chair across from the family.

"First of all," I said, "I'd like to offer my condolences to you. This is an extremely hard thing to face, especially during the holidays and from my heart I want you to know I'm very, very sorry. I think it's important for you to know that your husband and father did not suffer. He passed very quickly." I lied, but it made no sense to say otherwise.

"I also wanted you to know that I'm a registered paramedic and it's my opinion that the Security team that responded did so in exemplary fashion. They displayed professional behavior in their actions and response time to this emergency."

I answered a couple more questions and then there was nothing more to say. I got up to leave and when I got to the door, the daughter came over and gave me a big hug. "Thank you," she said.

It surprised me that I had tears running down my cheeks and all of a sudden it was very difficult to speak. "I'm so sorry. I tried everything I knew, but without equipment, I'm so sorry, I tried." Now I was openly crying.

"Thank you," she said again, "for not only trying, but for treating our father with respect and compassion; it was very kind of you. We feel a sense of relief that everything possible was done to try to save his life. For that we're very grateful."

"How do you know?" I asked.

"Because," she said, "I'm a good judge of character. Also, when I'm standing here looking into your eyes, I know you're telling me the truth."

"Well," I said, "I lost my father not too long ago, so I can say I know what you're going through. And I'll tell you it does get better. Take care in your heart; listen to your heart because he's there now. He'll be there always."

With that, I left. Later that night, one of the guys I work with came up to me and said, "Is it true?"

"Is what true?" I asked.

"Is it true you finally killed somebody with one of your farts?"

You know, that's what I loved about that crew, and I just had to laugh.

CHAPTER 18

STRANDED

B y now you've noticed that not every story takes place on the stage; however, they are all connected to a crew member in one way or another. And it wouldn't be right if I didn't include this one.

On this night, Allen D. and a good friend of his got into his semi-new car and headed out of town. Forty or so miles later on a long, quiet stretch of highway, Allen's car broke down.

The two of them walked up the road a ways and off to the left was a small dirt road. Allen and his friend discussed the matter for a few minutes and decided that the best thing to do would be to push the car onto the dirt road a ways so that it wouldn't be easily seen from the highway. Then, the next night after work, he'd get a couple of friends together and go out, get the car and bring it back to town.

By the time the show was over the following evening, Allen had recruited about five or six of us to go with him. Myself, I thought it would be fun to do a lot of drugs, drink a few beers, and go there with my good friends, which we all were. Transportation was a problem until Mike N. offered to drive everyone out in his VW van, complete with moon roof.

After we had checked our supplies, we all hopped into Mike's van and down the road we went. As we were approaching the area where Allen had left his car, he was saying how deserted this road was. Finally he said, "Slow down Mike, that's the dirt road."

Mike made a slow turn onto the dirt road and proceeded to drive down it.

Allen said, "It was right here; we didn't push it that far."

Mike stopped the van and we all piled out. Max said, "Look, there's fresh tire marks farther up the road. Let's walk a spell."

Another hundred yards up the road we found Allen's car. Someone had towed the car far enough down the dirt road to ensure they wouldn't be caught when they dismantled the car.

It was up on blocks. All four tires were gone. The trunk was open, cleaned out. The whole interior of the car was gutted and the engine was gone. All that was left was a shell of a car. I know I was stunned. "Holy shit, Allen. Damn, brother. I don't know what to say; this is really terrible."

All Allen did was walk around the car a couple of times, then walk back to the van where he said, "Fuck it. It's no big deal; my insurance will cover it. I'll just get a new one."

With all of us back in the van again, we smoked a couple more joints and someone said, "Hey, there's a whorehouse right down the road, let's go there for a while."

First of all, I'd never been to a brothel before, but I figured now was as good a time as any to see what one looked like; also, I didn't want the other guys to know that I was a virgin in that respect, so I said, "Fine, let's go!"

Only one small problem—none of us had plans to do this, so between all of us, we had about fifty bucks, hardly the big spenders that they were used to.

One guy finally made a deal with the girls while the rest of us waited in the bar area. We played pool, drank some beers, but it didn't take long before we got rowdy and were asked to please leave. Because we weren't there to cause any trouble, we did so quietly.

Half an hour later, Mr. Stud Man came out and we all hopped in the van once again to drive back home. A couple of miles down the road Max, who had brought a box with him, now opened it and took out a 22-caliber pistol. He stood up through the moon roof and proceeded to fire round after round into the night. Even though we were totally blitzed, we all realized that this was not a good idea. Mike was getting really pissed at Max. He pulled over to the side of the road and said, "Max, either put the gun away or walk. It's your choice."

Max made a quick decision and put the gun away. "Okay, all right, Mike; the gun's in the box, you big pussy."

Mike turned around, put the van in gear and started to drive again, but the engine started to sputter and spit. Then it died out and we came rolling to a stop. After a good hour of trying everything we knew how to do, we gave up. The van was not going to start and now there were six of us stuck there in the middle of the desert.

We had worn out our welcome at the whorehouse, so that left us two options. One, try to hitch a ride—but who in their right mind would pick up six crazed-looking men in the middle of the desert? Two, we could walk to the main freeway, about twelve miles away, where we could split up and stand a much better chance of getting a ride.

Let me tell you, five miles is a long way to walk; twelve miles is a journey. By the time we reached I-15 it was about 9:30 in the morning and already over 100 degrees hot. We'd sobered up a bit by now, but we looked like we felt—shit.

Bob said, "All right, here's where we split up. Mike, Darryl and I will go on ahead. Max, Al and Phil, you guys wait about thirty minutes; by that time we should get rides easier."

Yeah, but by that time it'll be 110 degrees out here and, oh well I thought, what the hell difference did thirty minutes make? Sure enough, they got a ride almost immediately, so we didn't even have to wait. We just started to hitchhike right away. But after twenty-five minutes or so, no cars had stopped; none had even slowed down.

By chance I looked behind me one time and Max, who was bringing up the rear, was flipping the bird to every car that passed us, not even knowing if they intended to stop or not.

"Goddamn, Max," Allen said. "Have you always been this retarded? You and Phil hide over there off to the side of the road. I'll get us a ride."

True to his word, Allen had a car stopped and was frantically waving for us to hurry up and get to the car. The driver was an old man about seventy or so in a small white compact, and as Max and I ran up to the open passenger door, I could hear him telling Allen, "Yeah, but where did those guys come from? I just saw you standing there; I didn't see them."

As Max and I quickly jumped into the back seat Allen asked him, "Uh, how old are you? They were standing right next to me. Are you sure you can see well enough to drive?"

We really were grateful and told him so. His air conditioning barely worked but it felt great to us. We had it made. I just slid back down in the seat and closed my eyes to take a little nap. Suddenly I heard Max go, "Oh my God, what's this?" Max had noticed a blanket covering the floor of the back of the car. When he lifted it up and peeked under it, he saw piles of Playboy and Penthouse magazines and God only knows what else. I was thinking, "Max, just shut up and don't say anything." But it was too late.

Max was saying, "Hey, man, are these your magazines? You must be a pervert. Look at all this shit!" Meanwhile the old man was saying no, those weren't his and he didn't know how they got there. But Max just wouldn't let up. "Hey, look at this. Isn't that pretty?" Now Max was holding up pictures for all of us to see.

Twenty miles outside of Vegas is an exit off I-15 called Apex. There is nothing out that way except an old gypsum mine, and I'm pretty sure this guy didn't work there. "Well," the old man said, "This is my turnoff. Sorry I couldn't take you all farther."

He turned on the Apex exit, drove a little ways, and stopped and let us out. Thanks, Max. So we all piled out and I gotta tell ya, I almost kicked Max right square in the balls. It was hot now, really hot, as we watched our ride drive down the road. Of course it was no big surprise when, five minutes later, the little old man came driving by at about eighty miles an hour and turned back on I-15 heading back into Vegas.

Damn, Max, do you ever shut up? We just started walking, not even trying to get a ride. We heard a honking sound and it was Mike in his mom's car, come to save the day. I'll tell you, in my eyes he did.

CHAPTER 19

THE SHRINKING DOOR

During my time at the scenery shop, we had some funny things happen. At the time, this was not humorous but, like many things, in hindsight it was pretty funny.

It seemed like the big shows that we built usually followed the same pattern. For the first couple of weeks or so, construction went at a steady pace; however, the final week was always hectic. Changes in the scenery, items added on, little things led to eighteen-hour days and a frantic pace.

Now I can't remember the particular show, but we were in the final week and it was the same story—long hours, the whole bit. I can remember looking up at this one particular set piece and I was thinking, "That's big; in fact, I think that's the biggest piece that we've ever built in this shop." It was massive.

Because of some design problems, it was decided to build this piece last. It wasn't unusual for the carpenters to work on a project right up until the truck came to pick it up for delivery, and even then the paint might be wet and the glue not dried yet.

It was going to be close. The truck was coming at 7:00 a.m. Friday morning; it was well past midnight and we had a lot to do. The hours passed. At 6:30 the final touches were applied and the long night was over. All we had to do was roll this big sucker over to the big roll-up doors and onto the truck; then we could all go home.

The truck arrived, a huge flatbed. They'd been doing this for years; the driver backed the flatbed up to the door perfectly. The trailer and the loading dock matched up. Now all that was left was to push this baby out the door and onto the trailer. Five minutes, tops.

Everybody in the shop joined in. We all gathered around and started to push. It moved slowly at first, but soon we had it coasting through the shop toward the big door. Almost to the door I let up a little bit, just barely pushing. I looked over at the guy next to me; we were bullshitting about something when the next thing I knew, my face smashed into the set. The set piece had come to such an abrupt stop that I had walked right into the back of it and then was knocked right on my butt.

"What the fuck was that?" I asked my friend. "What happened?"

My friend, who was holding his forehead, looked at me and said, "Well, off the top of my head, and that's no pun, I'd say the piece didn't clear the door."

"Didn't clear the door?" I said, still not understanding.

"Yeah, the piece is too big, you dumb shit. It won't go out the door."

Picking myself up off the ground I said, "No shit, that was dumb, who did that?"

"I don't know," he said, "but I sure wouldn't want to be that person."

Well, that piece was late that day. Even if they took the wheels off it was still three inches too high. They had to cut it down, cut the whole top off and weld it back together outside, then replace all the wood and do a couple of other things. I can tell you that I never saw that happen again; if it did, nobody said anything.

CHAPTER 20

CAUTION: THIS MEDICATION MAY MAKE YOU DROWSY. DO NOT MIX WITH ALCOHOL OR OPERATE HEAVY EQUIPMENT

As I look back over the years of partying and craziness that we were so fortunate to live through, I was amazed, then ashamed, of the role I played in much of it. But at the time you could not have given us any warning or advice, because we simply would not have listened to you. Years later I would finally face up to the fact that I was one of the biggest offenders.

I wasn't a pusher—none of us were. We were just guys who loved to do drugs and had enough money to buy what we wanted with enough left over to share with our buddies. However, when everyone did that, it meant that there were massive amounts of drugs around, plenty for everyone. And people did make mistakes. Thank God no one was killed.

Of course Quaalude, 714, was our favorite drug of choice with cocaine a close runner-up. But we weren't picky. So when I got the call from a friend of mine informing me that he had a supply of Seconal pills, I said sure, I'd take some off his hands. I ended up with a couple of hundred of these little pills. They were made to look like a certain brand of aspirin, complete with the arrow imprinted on one side. They were potent little bastards but they took a long time to kick in.

I heard more than once, "Hey, I don't feel anything yet, let me take another one." And of course I'd do it.

Dennis H. was not your usual stagehand; in fact, he was really out of place. Dennis was at home in the woods or living in the middle of the desert mining for gold, pretty much of a loner. The only thing we had in common was an intense desire to party.

Now Dennis didn't want to admit that he couldn't keep up with the rest of us, and that caused him a small amount of trouble from time to time.

One night in between shows, four or five us headed over to my house to adjust our attitudes. We smoked some pot, ate a couple of pills, and washed it all down with some liquor. We all headed back to the hotel to do the second show, just like we'd done so many times before.

We knew we all had a good buzz going on but we should have realized Dennis was a little more messed up than the rest of us when, halfway through the second show, we heard a loud commotion onstage.

Dennis had a long-running personality clash with one of the other guys onstage. I got there just in time to see Dennis wrap one of the curtains around the guy, then proceed to beat him about the head and body with his fists. We didn't want to interfere at first, because we figured that the guy had it coming. But after a minute or two it was obvious that Dennis had him wrapped up pretty good and, judging by the screams that were now coming from the curtain, well, it was time to step in and put an end to this whipping.

Dennis was upset as the other guy went limping back to the other side of the stage. "Damn it you guys, I was just getting fired up. I hate that little fucker."

We kept a close eye on Dennis the rest of the show to make sure he didn't attack anyone else. After the show Dennis made a half-hearted attempt to chase the other fellow, but once again we intervened, which allowed the guy to escape a second beating that night.

Dennis got into his truck and roared out of the parking lot. Colleen, who worked as wardrobe in our show, was also leaving to go home. She pulled out right behind Dennis. These two didn't particularly like each other but then, like I said, Dennis was a different breed so he had a limited circle of friends at the show.

As they pulled up to an intersection a mile or so from the Tropicana, Dennis was behind Colleen. When the light suddenly changed to red, she stepped on the brakes pretty hard. Dennis, however, thought she was going to try to make the light and he'd follow right behind her. He plowed right into the back of her.

Dennis in all probability was going to jail to spend the night, and I'm sure that it didn't help to tell the police, "That bitch shouldn't be allowed to drive. Anyone who drives like that shouldn't be allowed to have a license, even to breastfeed. Why, she shouldn't even be allowed to reproduce, the dumb c—t." Do not pass. Go. Go directly to jail.

The next night Dennis wanted to ask Colleen just what was her problem. Fortunately, we talked him out of it. God, what a snapper head. But we never considered that it was the pills that were the problem. They were just one of the many drugs we indulged in on a daily basis.

Then two nights later Allen, after taking two or three of the pills, ran into the back of a guy named Gene D. who performed in a specialty act during the Folies show. Luckily for Allen, Gene was pretty drunk at the time and thought it was funny. Allen told Gene he was sorry and to prove it, he'd take Gene to his favorite bar, where they ended up drinking and exchanging stories until the sun came up.

Then I almost had a car accident, so I decided that these little pills were not good for us. I got rid of them. Too bad I didn't feel the same way about all the other drugs we were doing at the time, but that would come years later.

CHAPTER 21

RACE FOR THE COKE

While I was on leave from the Trop, filming the "Crime Story" television series, it just so happened that an organization, who shall remain nameless forever, was about to put on its annual fair. It's a big fair, the biggest one all year. This particular year, they decided to have a contest in which the contestants would have to build a three-wheeled tricycle. Then, if it met all the requirements, it could be entered into a race. The racecourse was an oval and each lap was between a quarter and a half-mile long. It would be a relay race, so after each lap was completed, a new rider/driver would take over for the next lap. Four laps and the race would be completed.

Just to make things interesting, this organization made the first place prize one thousand dollars. One of the sponsor's officer was a gentleman by the name of Dave S., who also just happened to work on the rail. He mentioned to a couple of crew members that they should look into entering the race.

It's true that we were a group of misfits who liked to party big time; however, that fact didn't take away from another fact. And that was, we had some extremely talented people working backstage. Mike N. was one of those people, a guy who could and still can do anything with steel and wood. He was just one among many talented people who just happen to like to build things.

Now I never saw the trike in person but I did see photos. Obviously, it had three wheels, but that's where the similarities with the other trikes that were built ended. Unlike the other trikes, this one had a long extended front end. The front tire was small compared to the large rear tires. The chain from the front tire sprocket was also long; it was specially made to accommodate the extra length of the bike. The other unmistakable feature was the position the rider would assume. The other trikes positioned the rider in a top position. On the Trop's trike, the rider was almost in a laying down position in a seat that was only inches off the ground.

The other big factor was that we were all young guys in great shape. We'd all hung together for years, and much of that time was spent working out and running.

Race day came and the guys were pumped. It was no contest. I wasn't able to attend but the Trop crew won hands down; in fact, the whole day of the race was not spent on discussing race strategy but rather on how they were going to spend the money. They were confident bastards—and, as they proved, rightly so. The prize was collected and two days later the racing crew had come to agree on what they would do with their prize.

A party. They would throw a huge party.

One of the guys found a cabin that could be rented for a weekend. But a thousand dollars was a lot of money and even with all the deposits and rental fee, there was still a healthy surplus of cash. It was finally and, I might add, easily agreed that they would buy a quarter ounce of coke and whatever was left would go toward liquor.

A week later I got an invitation to a mountain bash. By then I'd heard all about the race, the victory, but the party was new information to me. Since I knew these guys and I've always loved the mountains, this was one party I wasn't going to miss.

Getting the night off was easy enough, so I made a date and told her that we'd be spending the night. I was careful with my selection because I wasn't sure how crazy it would get and I wasn't going to leave because my date couldn't hang with us. I didn't have to worry on that account.

Saturday morning arrived and I was up early, excited and ready to go. Cindy, my date, was waiting by the door when I drove up.

Good girl. She got in the car, leaned over and kissed me. It was a kiss that promised good things to come. As we finished the kiss and our tongues were parting, she lightly scraped hers over my teeth. "There," she said. "I just gave you a little surprise."

An hour later when I was starting to feel little electric tingles, she confirmed what I was already beginning to suspect. With her greeting kiss, she had slipped a hit of acid into my mouth. Not a minute too soon, we arrived at the cabin, for by now I was really coming on strong to the LSD.

That time of year, the middle of October, all the trees were in the process of changing colors, the sky was a brilliant blue, and everything else was green and beautiful.

We stood outside the car for a moment and then both started giggling. Cindy looked at me with those killer eyes and said, "I don't want to go in yet; in fact, I've got a little confession to make."

"What's that, baby?" I asked.

"I'm really horny, and I think we need to start this day out in a special way," she answered.

For the first time I noticed she had a big blanket under her arm and a bottle of wine in the other hand. We had all day and all night, so I took the blanket and wine and she kissed me again, then put her arm around my waist as we walked down the road a ways and ducked into the woods. We found a spot next to a little stream and laid the blanket out. Two hours later we remembered the party. It was now time to go mingle.

When we got back to the cabin, quite a few people had arrived. Now we could hear music drifting through the air. As we stepped up to the front door, it flew open and I found myself in the grip of a big bear hug.

"Hey Allen," I gasped, "It's great to see you." Allen, who was a really close friend, grinned back. He was very short in the hair department, but for some reason he seemed to have a full head of hair. It took me a minute to realize he had a towel over his head, and when I did, it just cracked me up. I looked over at Cindy and said, "You know, this is some really great acid."

The cabin was small, just a kitchen and living room downstairs and a bedroom and small loft upstairs. Allen led us upstairs and told us to sit down by a table, then sat down across from us. On the table was a bunch of weed, some pills, and a good-sized Tupperware bowl with a lid. We lit up a joint and just talked for a few minutes.

We started to get up to go downstairs when Allen stopped us, motioning for us to sit again. He then pushed the covered bowl over and with it a straw, razor blade, and a small mirror. I popped the lid off and inside the bowl was a pile of cocaine that was all crystal and rocky. A sign of good quality coke, but I was amazed at how much there was.

"Everyone who comes up here is on the honor system," Allen said. "Enjoy." He got up and went downstairs.

Cindy and I helped ourselves, then stood up to go downstairs. The small downstairs area was packed by now, and in our state of mind we decided the outdoor deck would be a better place for us. We were seated in one corner of the deck and for hours we talked with all the people who came out there.

Then, late in the afternoon, we were sitting all alone and we noticed that it had become cloudy and, in fact, it had been raining for a while. She took me by the hand and led me back into the cabin. But she didn't stop; she went right out the front door and back to the car. "Please get the blanket and let's go back by the stream." You didn't have to ask me twice.

Back by the stream, Cindy magically produced another bottle of wine and a big fat joint. Now I know acid can alter one's perception in drastic measures, but the weather was almost eerie. The clouds had dropped really low; in fact, we were in the clouds. A fine mist enveloped us, dampening all sounds around us except for the soft flowing sounds of the small creek beside us. It felt prehistoric. Cindy must have felt the same way because she laughed, then looked over at me and said, "Can't you hear it? We'll see it any second now."

"Hear what, baby, what do you hear?" I asked.

"The big dinosaur, a T-Rex, it'll be coming through the mist any second now," Cindy answered.

"Well," I said, "Let's play cave man." And I literally tore her clothes off her body.

Later the mist cleared, the clouds parted, and golden rays of sunshine filtered through the trees. Our senses were electric with the feeling; I swear we even felt the colors around us.

"Cindy," I said, "That is the best acid I've taken. This has been quite an experience."

She said, "Kiss me," and with that, she gave me a second hit of the LSD. We got up and started to get dressed.

"You know Phil, you were devastating just now and your passion is commendable; however, it leaves me with a small problem, baby."

"Oh, and what is that?" I asked.

"It appears that my blouse has no buttons left on it. In fact, it doesn't even look like a blouse anymore. And I can't find my underwear either," Cindy remarked.

"Oh, sorry, really I mean it. Did you bring any other clothes?"

"Yep, they're in the car."

"Well, we could wrap you up in the blanket till we get back there," I said.

Back at the cabin, well, it was chaos. After being in a quiet, intimate setting, the cabin by comparison was a madhouse. The place was packed, with a hundred different conversations going on all at once. I looked at Cindy and without saying a word we both went right out to the porch again. Some time later Cindy said she was thirsty, so I went inside to get us something to drink.

In the kitchen I met Allen again and he was just as toasted as I was. With drinks in my hands, I was starting to leave when a fellow walked in with a medium-sized brown paper bag. He set it on the counter and removed a bowl, which was covered, very similar to the one upstairs. Wow, more blow, was the thought that came to mind. I looked at Allen and I could see that he, too, was curious.

The answer to that curiosity came in the most unusual way. The guy accidentally dropped the bowl. Mushrooms. Magic mushrooms. Not for even a moment did Allen or I think the guy was a chef and had come up here to cook us a meal. I've got to tell you that Allen truly had the reflexes of a cat. Holding the container by the lid was a costly mistake. Thinking back, it's amazing how fast the two of us identified the contents of the bowl, and Allen was on the floor scooping them up before the bowl hit the ground. A second later I joined him.

The guy's reaction time was pretty bad, which worked against him. By the time he was able to say anything, Allen was on his second, maybe even third, mouthful of those succulent, potent mushrooms. I had both hands full, but Allen had the right idea: no giving them back once he swallowed them.

The guy was frantic. "No, no, hey stop that, stop it you guys. Do you guys hear me? Stop it. Those aren't mine. I mean they're mine but I gotta sell them."

His pleas fell on deaf ears. The guy might as well have been speaking Chinese because Allen didn't even look up at the guy; he just kept on eating. I, on the other hand, looked up at the man and all of a sudden I realized what we were doing and sort of felt sorry for him. That was, until he grabbed Allen.

He was really upset by now, with half of his precious shipment of mushrooms either devoured or in our possession. This constituted a major financial loss on his part. Since it appeared to him that neither Allen nor I were paying attention to his pleas, he finally reached out and grabbed Allen by his shirt collar and tried to pull him back, away from his mushrooms.

Obviously, Allen was not an acquaintance of his, because if he knew Allen he wouldn't have done that. I had to laugh because it was a classic case of man versus animal. The first pull on Al's collar was just a little tug; Al didn't even feel it. The second tug was a bit harder; this Allen acknowledged with a low grunt.

In the distressed state the guy was in, his third hard yank damn near tore Allen's collar completely off his shirt. Allen barely glanced up, then swatted his hand away.

"Fuck, what's the matter with you man, are you crazy?" the guy said. "You hurt my arm, you son of a bitch." He was cradling one arm, with a genuine look of pain etched on his face.

Still Allen didn't say a word; he looked like a pit bull that was challenging another dog to try and take his bone. There were pieces of mushrooms at the corners of his mouth and in his hair, and his hands were covered with juice. He truly looked evil.

"Uh, listen buddy," I said. "You're talking to a guy who once told me that he got real fucked up one night passed out on his bed. He remembered being terribly hungry during the middle of the night but he thought he'd gotten up and eaten something. Well, late the next morning when he woke up, he found what had been a frozen turkey in bed with him, and a good portion of one leg had been eaten. So if I were you, I'd consider what my options are at this point. Are these mushrooms really worth getting hurt over?"

Still holding his arm he looked at me, then at Allen, and he shivered like he just caught a glimpse of a dangerously insane person (how perceptive). Then he looked back at me. "I guess I don't have much choice, do I?" he said.

"Look," I said. "I imagine you're out a good amount of cash, so how about I give you some money? I didn't bring a lot, but I'll give you most of it. And here, why don't you eat a few?" I handed him what I had in one hand.

Mushroom Man left the kitchen as Al was getting to his feet.

"God, Al, how many handfuls did you eat?"

"Not enough," Al said. "I haven't seen mushrooms around here for quite a while. I didn't make a pig of myself, did I? I mean, do you think I was rude?"

"Rude? Al, that guy's not sure you can even talk; your being rude didn't even occur to him. You should go clean up; you're a mess."

After that, the rest of the night is sort of hazy. I know that sometime during the night a group of naked people came outside. Soon they were running around the cabin and the surrounding woods. Cindy and I were tucked away in one corner of the porch. Our bed consisted of a queen size air mattress on which we piled our sleeping bags. I had also brought a large tarp to cover us just in case of rain.

The night passed slowly, but sooner or later everyone noticed that sunrise was approaching. Some people were starting to crash; others were lying around in groups, quietly talking among themselves. The party was winding down fast and after having a great time, it was kind of sad. It was time to go. We thanked everyone, asked if there was anything we could do, then loaded our things in the car and headed for home.

As we were passing the place where the small stream was located, Cindy said, "Phil, please pull over for a moment. I'd like to stop and get a drink of that cool water." Lying on the bank with our faces close to the water, Cindy let out a small giggle that turned into a deep lusty sigh. She turned her head toward me and gently brushed her lips on mine. Her eyes seemed to question me.

"What?" I asked.

"I was just wondering, ah, I don't suppose you feel like playing cave man again, do you?" she asked.

It was my turn to giggle.

CHAPTER 22

FEEDING FRENZY

Ever since I've been a stagehand, it seems as though I've known by instinct that food and stagehands are synonymous. When it comes to convention work (that is, putting in a large trade show), or in showrooms where they engage in star policy, doing weekly show changes, the smartest thing that any client can do is start out the day by providing the crew with donuts and coffee. This simple act serves some important functions.

The stagehand is fed; it's a well-known fact that stagehands begin a search for food the instant the job begins. If you watch a crew begin work and it hasn't been fed, you can observe this behavior quite easily. The stagehands with little experience do this very awkwardly; to a seasoned veteran it's embarrassing. Now on the other hand, a veteran will do his work, never appearing to have any other motive than doing the task at hand. But by break time the veteran will have already made contact with and arranged to be fed by anyone who can provide food and drink.

If you're the client and you're going to provide lunch for the crew, it's best if you don't let them see the food until the last possible moment. There's nothing worse than bringing out the food early. The crew will stop working and start hovering over the food like vultures.

We're pretty much pack rats; there will be no food left to clean up. Anything we can't eat we take and store for later. That's because you never know how long a work call may last. Also, if you don't have to spend money on food later, say during the next break, it's all the better. The fact is that the only time any food is left on the serving tray is when it's so bad that a dog wouldn't eat it.

This one particular call that took me to the stage at Caesar's Palace was quite unique. It seems that a company ran into a jurisdiction problem over how the crew was to be allowed to work; specifically, the use of the company's crew to work the show crossed over into our union's jurisdiction and our guys were not called into work, when they had every right to the jobs.

The business agent went down to Caesar's and struck a deal with the company. It was decided that the union would match man for man to their crew up to 50% of the crew. So if they had 25 people on the out-of-town crew, they would have to employ 13 people from the union as standbys. Because of the technical nature of their show, it only made sense that their crew would do the work. In fact, it was the only way that the show would be installed on time. So as standbys we were told to help unload the trucks, uncrate the equipment, and then basically sit down, shut up and stay out of the way.

There were a lot of old-timers on the call because the dispatcher from the union knew that whomever he sent out was going to get paid for doing nothing during the whole show. It would turn out to be a thousand-dollar freebee over two days. I asked one of the old-timers how it was that I got the call and he said that the dispatcher probably had filled the call with as many older members as possible, then filled the rest of the slots with the guys who had reputations as hard workers and who never turned down work calls, even when they knew the job would be shitty—one of the few times he could show his appreciation to them. Cool.

After the little work we could do was done, we did what we were told: picked a spot upstage and gathered together, staying out of the way. Two and a half hours later, when their crew took its first break, they enjoyed the usual coffee and donuts; however, they were not very considerate of their standby buddies who, while sitting for all that time doing nothing, had worked up quite an appetite. They left us nothing to eat and that was a big mistake.

By the time the lunch break was approaching, there was a group of starving stagehands huddled in a group. Then the most miraculous thing happened. Out of nowhere appeared a waiter with a food cart full of sandwiches and drinks. These were the fancy ones with the crusts cut off and little toothpicks through the centers. First class all the way.

I looked over at one of the old-timers and said, "I'm not gonna go hungry this time; I'm getting me some food."

As I started to get up, he put a hand on my shoulder and said, "Wait until the dessert cart comes." Sure enough, a minute later the dessert came; then the waiter left.

"Now," he said, and we got up and made our way to the food.

The way we ate, you could compare it to throwing a wounded seal in the path of a killer whale. In two or three minutes the carts were empty. Dirty plates and empty crumpled soda cans littered the carts; it looked like a crime scene. In a way, it was. With full bellies and our thirst quenched, we retired to our little spot. You could hear the satisfied belches and the occasional fart, our compliments to a dedicated chef. Someone actually suggested calling housekeeping and putting in a request for pillows so we could take a nap—a joke, thank God.

The working crew was given the word to break for lunch. As they walked over to the lunch carts a collective "What the hell?" could be heard.

These guys who worked for the company, as we found out, were underpaid in comparison to our pay scale and instead of having rooms at Caesar's, as is the usual practice, they were housed at the King's Eight down the road. Three or four people occupied a room; some guys were sleeping on rollaway beds. All these little cost-cutting measures were taken by a company with the sole purpose of being as cheap as possible. Their workers were being treated badly, in our opinion. They were given no per diem in compensation of the hardships one experiences when working away from home.

So, considering all these things, it's no wonder that when they saw the food was all gone, they were a little pissed. "Who ate all the goddamn food? They feed us three times a day and somebody just ate our lunch. What the fuck is going on?"

It only took a minute for their boss to come over to see what the commotion was all about. Now here was a guy who could get angry. He felt that a crime had been committed and he was just the one to get to the bottom of this injustice. It didn't take a super sleuth to solve the mystery. Twenty stagehands still licking their lips, their bellies round and extended, and barely able to stay awake, well, it was painfully obvious where the food had gone.

Of course as we lay there watching the whole scene unfold, we realized it was just a matter of time before we were going to get a stern talking-to. I got up to go to the bathroom just as the boss started to come over to confront us.

"You there, go sit down for a minute. I've got something to say to you all."

I went back and sat down with an expression on my face that said, "What in the world is all this about? Did we do something wrong? How could we have done anything wrong just sitting there like we were?"

The boss then began to vent his anger. "You guys are really something. Our crew is working their asses off to get this show in on time. They only get this one lunch break because we're under the gun. We try to provide them with a nice lunch and before they get a chance to enjoy it, you lazy overpaid excuses for a bunch of pigs eat all their food. You all should be ashamed, just ashamed of yourselves. Not only will these guys miss their meal, but you've also caused the company a hardship that, frankly, we don't need right now. You guys are a shameful representation of your union."

But our skins were thick and I know, speaking for myself, it took everything I had to appear ashamed—to produce a tear was completely out of the question.

From somewhere in the back of our group, someone asked, "Does that mean tomorrow we should bring a box lunch?" I never claimed that we were a brilliant group of people; in fact, there have been many studies that prove the larger the group, the lower the mentality.

Where stagehands are concerned you can multiply that statistic by a factor of two.

The boss was so angry he lost his ability to yell at us. He did the only thing he could do; he just stomped away.

One of the old-timers said, "Boys, I believe we've crossed the line here and I suggest we agree on a way we can redeem ourselves before we have a situation here we can't handle. We did do a shitty thing here."

So we took up a collection among us; then we chose two crew members who had the unenviable task of approaching the boss and asking him if we might amend the situation we'd created by letting a couple of guys go out and buy lunch for the working crew.

Their boss gave his consent and we did all we could to obtain pardon for ourselves and our despicable behavior. In the end we were able to eliminate most of the bad feelings we'd created, but that didn't mean we could be careless the next day, and we knew it. From that time on, the waiter had specific instructions to guard the food until the boss told him otherwise.

I, for one, brought my lunch the next day.

CHAPTER 23

THE PARTY

My friends and I had been working night after night and the routine was becoming very monotonous. With no holiday in the near future, we were getting very bored.

I had recently moved into a one-bedroom apartment with a loft. Very quickly we invented a game which consisted of kicking a soccer ball as hard as we could, with the idea of putting the ball upstairs with an amazing kick from the downstairs area, and vice versa. That was it—basically just kicking the shit out of this ball. Every picture, every wall decoration was blasted off the walls. Every object on my tables was either shattered or in pieces on the ground. After a session with the ball, the neighbors were yelling and screaming; they probably thought murder was being committed on more than one occasion.

One night after the ball went crashing through the front window, we decided we'd have to cool it while the maintenance man came over to deal with the damage. So while we were waiting for the emergency repairs to be completed, the topic of a party came up.

After discussing all the alternatives regarding location, it became clear that my place was the most desirable. The main reason was that ten feet from my back sliding glass door was the entrance to the largest of three pools that served the apartment complex. The more we discussed the details involved, the more the choice became clear that my place was the best, hands down.

The next thing I had to do was get permission from the

apartment complex managers to allow me to have this event. It quickly became apparent that party-throwing was not high on their list, so they constructed a few hurdles that in their estimation I would not be able to overcome. However, they didn't realize who they were dealing with.

The one stipulation they insisted on (which they felt confident would be the party stopper) was that if I was going to have a party, I couldn't make the pool area off-limits to anyone who was a rent paying resident; therefore, if I was willing to extend an invitation to the entire complex, some five hundred-plus units, then I could have the party. I told them that I'd have an answer the next day.

That night at work I told my buddies what the deal was and that it would be a great help if they could chip in toward some of the expenses. Not a problem. I now had the green light.

Back in the manager's office the following day, I just had to mess with them a little.

"It's just not fair that you guys would make having a party all but impossible. Do you realize the cost involved when you insist I invite the whole complex? What do you have against a few people having fun?" I asked.

"We're just trying to be fair; however, no one has had a party yet, and we like it that way."

"So if I actually could have invited all those people, I'd have been in business, huh?"

"Yep, then you'd have been in business, son."

"Okay, I just wanted to make sure I understood the rules, and now that I do, I'd like you to see something." I opened the door and retrieved a two-foot-by-two-foot poster I'd stashed behind a small bush before entering the office.

It read: "The Party—come join in the food, the drinks, and whatever else is present in honor of the first party ever held at poolside in the history of this complex. Everyone is cordially invited. No, that's incorrect—attendance is mandatory. Enjoy the music, the water and the beautiful women. Gates open from 6:30 till? PS: Don't you dare forget your suit. If you do, you'll qualify for a special surprise!"

I guess I can go ahead and post these invitations, huh guys? You see, my friends and I have always enjoyed a challenge. But I'll tell you now, this isn't gonna be some half-assed party. We're going to feed people burgers, hot dogs, New York steaks and all the fixings. I give you my word that when the party is over, this place will be in better shape than before. One last thing, we'll do everything in our power to prevent any damage, and likewise, any type of violence will not be tolerated. There is one purpose for this party and that's fun. That's what we know how to do best.

The managers just smiled and nodded their heads. What could they say without looking like total idiots?

It took most of one day to buy all the food and drink and another whole day to set everything up. On the day of the party I invited a few people over for a special pre-party dinner. I made a meal called Bonya Cota, comprised of shrimp, filet mignon, six or seven different types of vegetables, and a butter and garlic sauce to kill for. It's a fun meal to cook and eat. Everything is placed on the table uncooked with electric frying pans spaced out so everyone is able to reach one easily. The only thing is, you can't let the sauce get too hot or the butter will burn, so one person is appointed to be responsible for a pan in their area.

One reason I like this meal is that it keeps people around the table for a long time. Everyone picks what they want to eat, then tosses those items into the pan. You pick an area in a pan and designate that as your area; other people should respect your area and the food you're cooking. They do, at first.

Sooner or later it always happens. You'll hear, "Hey, you just took my piece of shrimp. I thought you took a piece of my meat earlier but I didn't say anything, but I know that was my shrimp." Soon everybody's eating everybody else's food. It's not unusual to spend two or three hours at the table eating off and on. It also costs you about a half a case of good wine, too.

We had to wrap up the dinner as the 6:30 mark grew near and the first of the partygoers showed up.

I met so many people that evening. Since a good majority of my friends had to work the show that evening, I knew most of the early crowd were people who lived in the complex. At first there were little groups of people huddled together, obviously people who lived next to each other but who didn't feel comfortable mixing with the people they didn't know.

Well, I knew how to change that. I started up the music and announced, "The bar is now open and I'd like to ask a favor of everyone. As you get a drink, please write your first name on the nametags that are to the right of the bar. Keep your tags; each one is numbered and later in the evening we'll be having a few drawings for some neat gifts."

With nametags in place, the small groups started to dissolve as everybody felt more comfortable knowing the names of the other people.

As the sun disappeared and darkness prevailed, the party started to really get rolling. By nine o'clock the pool area was jam packed, people were starting to get in the pool, almost everyone was dancing, and those who weren't were either in line at the bar or getting food by the grills. There were five hundred and fifty numbered nametags by the bar and by ten o'clock they were gone. My friends hadn't even shown up yet and I knew when the second show ended, a hundred more people would show up at the very least; it could be a lot more.

Fluorescent lights provided the only lighting in the pool area. Around eleven the light seemed to dim and there was loud laughter and whistling coming from the pool. I made my way to poolside and was greeted by the sight of five or so young ladies sitting on guys' shoulders with wet t-shirts on that had now become transparent. Cool, nice bodies for the guys to enjoy, and more girls were jumping into the water each minute. I was enjoying this, no doubt about that, but then I remembered the managers. Just how open-minded were they, and would they come around at any moment and demand we stop the party? Couldn't worry about that now; in fact, I forgot about it almost as quickly as it had entered my mind.

One friend of mine came armed with four hundred Quaaludes, 714, the party drug of choice. I watched people so drunk and wasted they couldn't even work the gate latch to get out of the pool area.

When I think back, years later, I wonder if everybody made it home safely that evening. Did some leave and get in trouble with the police? Did anyone die that night? Of course, back then, those thoughts never even entered my mind.

Twelve midnight, and Security for the complex showed up at poolside. I finally was told they wanted to have a word with the host of the party. Walking up to these guys, I couldn't help noticing their attention was divided between the pool and the bar. I knew what was in the pool, a hundred or so naked people, but the bar? Could these guys be thirsty?

"Are you the host of the party?" one asked. "How late do you expect this to go on? It's hard to ignore, uh, those people in the pool. You know it's just a matter of time before our bosses find out and we may have to shut this thing down."

"What do you suggest I do?" I asked.

"Well, the music is pretty loud and so is the crowd; if you could tone it down a bit, that would probably help. My partner and I might be tied up way over at the other end of the complex and it wouldn't be the fist time we've experienced problems with our radios. I mean it's possible, you know what I mean?"

"Yes, I know exactly what you mean; as a matter of fact, I have a question of my own. Are either of you a drinking man?"

The older gentleman broke into a big smile and informed me that if I hadn't noticed by now, his last name was McKenzie, a man in a long line of McKenzies whose lines went back centuries in the land of the leprechauns; did that answer my question?

"Follow me," I said, and led them over to the bar. Renee, a former girlfriend of mine and a bartender by trade, was gracious enough to relieve me of the burden of pouring drinks. She stepped up and flashed that killer smile of hers and asked how she could be of service. This sparked a number of visions in my mind and she had to get my attention before I remembered why I was there.

"Let's see," I said as I looked at the older gentleman. "Wouldn't a glass of Chivas be nice?" He barely nodded. "Renee, please give me an unopened bottle of Chivas; make that two bottles.

"Johnny Walker Black Label is not bad either, in my opinion." Another nod. "Renee, two bottles of Black, please."

"My apartment is number 65, right over there," I pointed. "And it just so happens that in ten minutes or so I'll be going out the front door to take a load of garbage to the dumpster and what I can't fit in, I'll set behind it. Just thought you'd need to know that."

The transaction was well worth it. We never saw them for the rest of the night.

Twelve-thirty and now the show kids were starting to arrive. Three or four of the girls asked to use my shower to get clean after a night of dancing. Two of them suggested using it together and asked if I'd care to join them. Thank you, believe me I'm flattered; we should definitely talk about this another time. However, I need to be by the pool and be the gracious host I promised to be.

One-thirty and once again the pool area is packed. The fluorescent lights had been turned to a position in their fixtures that no longer allowed them to work. The pool itself was a collection of naked bodies that left little room to maneuver. The naked people were now also lying around the pool on the lounge chairs, and some were just sitting on the edge of the pool with their feet in the water. It seemed like someone had put a notice on the gate entering the pool area: "No clothes allowed past this point; no exceptions."

I was still in shorts when, close to two a.m., two Metro Police officers walked through the gate and asked to speak to the person in charge. Great, I thought, it was a great party while it lasted, and I knew that no matter what happened I'd get laid, so I made my way as quickly as possible over to the police in hopes I could stop them from getting any closer to the pool.

"Yes sir," I said. "I understand you want to speak to the person responsible for this mess. First of all, am I in trouble? Are you going to arrest me or something like that, because I really did try to keep a handle on things but things just…

"Sir, just hold up a minute, okay?" the officer said. "The primary reason we're responding to this location is that we just received the second complaint that the music is too loud. If you would consider turning down the music level, I think we could go, and as long as there are no more complaints, there shouldn't be any problems."

What amazed me was how these officers were willing to ignore the very scene that was happening before them; in fact, they were very careful to stand with their backs to the pool, attempt to deliver their message, and leave. Cool.

When they were leaving, the younger one said, "By the way, to your advantage, we think the same person made the call. When they wouldn't identify themselves we were able to use our discretion with much greater leeway, so please don't make us come out again."

"Yes sir." Interesting that someone would call and complain about the loud music but not about the hundred or so people that were naked and engaging in different levels of personal contact with one another. Go figure.

Come sunrise the hardest of partiers were beginning to wind down, so with the help of a couple of people, we spent the next hour cleaning up the mess we'd created, restoring the lighting fixtures to working condition, breaking down the bar and food tables, returning the pool chairs and lounges to their respective positions, and generally putting everything in order. When we were finished, you couldn't even tell we'd been there.

Later that morning when all the leftovers were stacked in my kitchen, we took an inventory just to see what had been consumed the night before. Here's what we came up with: nine 750-ml. bottles of Chivas Regal, six 750-ml. bottles of Johnny Walker Red, four 750-ml. bottles of Johnny Walker Black, six 750-ml. bottles of Smirnoff Vodka, and three 750-ml. of Beefeater's gin. We also finished off three 750-ml. bottles of Tequila Gold by Hosey, four cases of red wine and two cases of white wine, each with six bottles per case, and one bottle of Tuacwa (exclusively kept in the possession of one Andy Anderson, who I'm pretty sure didn't share with anyone). Then there were over one hundred New York steaks, forty pounds of baby back pork ribs, twelve pounds of potato salad, three pounds of macaroni salad (not a popular item I guess), ten large bags of tortilla chips, two gallons of salsa, ten large bags of barbeque chips, ten large bags regular chips, and five pounds of trail mix. And finally, twenty cases of Coke, twenty cases of Seven-Up, five cases of soda water, five cases of tonic, ten cases of Dr. Pepper and five gallons of orange juice. Well, that covers the major items. We had a couple of drawings where the winners got $15.00 gift certificates to an adult bookstore, a couple of tickets to our show, and a couple of gag gifts.

Before the party one of my friends suggested we put out a box so that if somebody wanted to give a couple dollars to help reduce our out-of-pocket expenses, they could. There was over $700.00 in the box when the party was over. Cool. Even today, when talking with guys with twenty or more years in the business, it's not uncommon for that evening to be talked about.

CHAPTER 24

BIG SHOTS

O ver the last quarter-century working for the Tropicana Hotel, I've seen ownership change hands four times. During one of those changeovers, the people selling had almost closed the deal and an extravagant party was planned to put the finishing touches on the buyers, a party where all parties concerned would be able to relax and iron out the last few details remaining.

For this party money was no expense; the fanciest table settings and decorations were ordered. A special chef was hired to put together a culinary meal that would rival any restaurant in the world. The beverages that were to be served also received the same scrutiny, ensuring only the best liquor would be served. About all that was left was decorating the room in which the party was to be held. To this day, I don't know whose responsibility it was to handle that end of things, but something went terribly wrong.

The story I heard was that a company in Los Angeles was contracted to decorate the room. Using some outrageous set design, the room was to be given a luxurious atmosphere along the lines of an elegant speakeasy, a 1920's feel. All the people working the party would be dressed accordingly; everything was planned to sweep the prospective buyers right off their feet.

Three days before the party the hotel received a call from L.A., and that single call caused more chaos than any other thing I can ever remember. The room decorations were not going to be delivered;

something had happened, but the bottom line was that the decorations had been destroyed. As if that wasn't bad enough, the company had nothing left to offer as a replacement. The panic quickly reached the hierarchy of the hotel.

The president and CEO of the Trop quickly evaluated any and all options and, when all else failed, contacted the hotel carpenters. Explaining the crisis at hand, the head hotel carpenter shook his head and told the president, "Our crew is sort of small. That problem we can overcome, but you don't have any plans, no blueprints, which makes this very difficult. The truth is, it wouldn't be right for me to promise you something I can't deliver."

"Well, we're in real trouble here. I don't suppose you have any suggestions, do you?"

The hotel carpenter thought for a minute, then said, "You know, there's a bunch of stagehands over in the showroom and this is kinda right up their alley. In fact, last year you should have seen the New York Central Park set and the mock storefront district they built for New Year's. It was really pretty. Have you talked to them yet?"

Within the hour, the president was speaking to a stagehand by the name of Bob. Bob had been building stage scenery for years and he knew every shortcut there is to know. Not only that, but he knew architecture from all different periods; plus, he knew the different influences that countries around the world developed throughout the centuries, which made certain types of architecture so recognizable. He was the best chance the hotel had. If Bob couldn't rescue the party, then no one could.

Before the first show he called us together and said, "This is serious; I don't know if we can actually pull this off, but if we do, it would be a really good thing. I don't want to shock you guys, but your reputation as stagehands in this hotel leaves much to be desired. In fact, a lot of people around here think you're a bunch of loaded, out of control jack offs. But I know different. When you guys put your minds to it, you're some of the hardest-working people I know and you're talented, too. I need everyone who works on my carpenter crew to commit the next two and a half days to me, no getting fucked up and not showing up for work, no leaving early. I'm going to need you guys to promise me one hundred and ten percent. If you can't, I can't take this job on. If you tell me you're all in, I know your word is good because not once have any of you ever lied to me. So what's it gonna be?"

We had done many jobs with Bob over the years and he was one of the best bosses we'd ever had, so of course we said yes.

Bob decided since the party was all about business deals and money, that he would do a bank theme. We would make the entrance look like a big vault door, which would swing on giant hinges. It would be as visually identical to the real thing as possible. As you walked inside, the walls immediately to the left and right would resemble the teller counters in a bank. Then along the right wall, all the way to the other end of the room, would be safety deposit boxes. On the left wall would be fake entrances to the bank president's office, VP's office and so on. The wall on the far end of the room opposite the entrance would once again resemble the tellers' counter.

At first the president didn't think the idea was too glamorous, but after looking at a few quick sketches which Bob drew for him, he was convinced.

Early the next morning Bob got things organized. Some of us were sent to get materials; others went to the Trop warehouse to make room to build and set up the table saws, the TCD saw for cutting steel, make sure we had gas for the welders—basically to get everything ready so the work could begin. Because the project happened so fast, there were no plans, no blueprints, nothing to go by. But Bob had it all worked out in his head. He would say, "Phil, this is what I need you to do." Then he would make a fast drawing on a piece of paper, at the same time explaining as he drew. "Do you understand? Good. Do it."

We worked from 7:00 in the morning until 6:30 that night and then we worked our two shows. After the shows, we went right back to the warehouse. We worked all night and most of the next day. At 3:30 that afternoon, we all went home, grabbed a nap and were back at 7:30 that night to work the shows.

One more day was all the time left. After the show Bob decided that it would be better for us to get some sleep, so he told us to be back at 6:00 a.m. He also called the Union Hall and requested ten more carpenters.

The work went smoothly and by 1:00 that afternoon the vault door was completed, the safety deposit box wall was done, and almost all the teller window/counter sections were built. Still there was much work to do; everything had to be painted and quite a bit of detail work needed to be done.

One of the things I'm sure Bob considered was that the showroom was dark that night (no shows), so we were not inconvenienced by having to stop the work. And work we did. Some of our wives got together and brought us a big meal. After that it was back to work.

Five-thirty the next morning Bob yelled out, "Clean up, put the tools away—we did it, boys." But that didn't mean the work was done. All the things we built still had to be transported to the hotel and installed. It had to be done by 4:30 that afternoon. With the president keeping a keen eye on us, still not sure we'd be able to deliver, he informed Bob that he'd provide the manpower to get everything over to the hotel and into the room. All we'd have to do is put it together. The crew grabbed a couple hours of sleep, then went back to work for the final push.

Bob smiled as the pieces of scenery were put together and bolted into place. It was a thing of beauty. It was not 1:30 in the afternoon and we were done. We all sat down and looked around the room. We were in the bank, no doubt about it.

Just then the president walked in and his jaw almost dropped to the floor. "Oh my God, this is truly an amazing sight." He'd been busy all day with the prospective buyers and hadn't been back to the room since earlier that morning. "I don't know what to say, guys. This is just unbelievable. I had no idea you guys were so talented. I assure you that I'm deeply indebted to you all. This is just wonderful."

He shook all our hands and turned to leave; then he stopped, turned back to us and said the most astonishing thing, at least to us. "This has meant so much to me, I take it personally. So if you guys would like to attend the party as my guests, I'd be honored. Your reputations aside, I'm sure you'd be on your best behavior. The dress is Black Tie."

Wow, we were shocked. The president of the hotel inviting a bunch of whacked-out misfit stagehands to be his guests at a party attended by some of the biggest people in the hotel industry—financiers who handled millions of dollars, lawyers from giant law firms specializing in putting together huge deals, and other top professionals in the industry whose purpose was to consummate this deal.

What did we have in common with these people? Not one thing. And that was what was so appealing about attending this party; we had to go. We made a quick decision that we would all go out and rent tuxedos, and wives and girlfriends were given permission to go out and buy new outfits and whatever else they needed. We were going all out, dressed to the nines, as the phrase goes.

A group of us met before the party at a bar downstairs and had a couple of drinks before heading upstairs. Speaking for myself, I experienced a moment of self-consciousness; like I said before, what did I have in common with any of these people? I knew nothing about their world. The last thing I wanted to do is come out looking like the uneducated person I really am. Perhaps the best thing to do was to just get a drink, sit down, and keep my mouth shut.

As we were greeted at the door by the party host, we were asked for our invitation. Oh, no! After all we went through, now a simple invitation stood in our way. We didn't want anything in any way to cause a commotion or draw attention to us, so we told the guy we were just curious about what was going on and we'd be leaving.

As we started to walk away we heard, "Wait a moment please, I've just been informed that you're on the invited guest list. I was unaware of who you were; my apologies. Please come in, ladies and gentlemen."

I kind of figured that being invited was a nice gesture on the president's part, but I also thought that in the scheme of things we'd probably be seated way off in the corner of the room where we'd be not so visible. I was wrong. Our table was right next to the president's and new buyers of the hotel. Once we were seated, the president came over and warmly greeted each of us and told us to enjoy ourselves, beginning with a visit to the bar.

Soon the room was packed; music livened things up and people were soon out on the dance floor. The atmosphere was relaxed and we found ourselves mingling with those around us. To my surprise, our conversations were light-hearted and easygoing. Evidently the business deal had gone through and now these people were here to relax.

A thing I've noticed over the years is that there is definitely a certain mystique surrounding my profession. Whenever anyone has asked what I do for a living, upon hearing the answer, the response is always something like, "Wow, that sounds really interesting; tell me more about what you do." Or, "Have you met any stars? Who were they?" Tonight was no different. When people found out what we did for a living, then found out we had built the scenery for the party, they were very impressed.

Even though it was suggested that we be on our best behavior, that didn't mean we couldn't have fun. People we'd met throughout the evening would stop by our table and listen to our jokes; in this business you hear about every joke known to man, so our table was becoming a popular spot. I noticed the president was now sitting at our table along with two or three of his guests. Next thing we knew, our tables were pushed together and a few minutes later we were joined by yet another table.

Time came for the dinner to be served and the president stood and raised his glass. "I would like to make a toast," he said. "To the new owners: I wish them success with their new investment. The Tropicana Hotel has long enjoyed the reputation of being 'the jewel of the Strip.' The employees here are proud of this hotel and are dedicated to making every visitor so comfortable that when they return to Las Vegas, they don't consider staying anywhere else but here with us.

"As long as I'm on the subject of employees, I'd like to introduce you to a group of them. As you entered this party tonight, if you're like me you probably said, 'Wow, look at this place; it looks fantastic.

It must have taken a good month or so to decorate this place.' Well, I must tell you, three days ago it appeared as if this party might be a big disaster. The company we contracted to do the decorations called us and told us they would not be able to do the job. Believe me, that was the worst news I've had in quite a while. However, these talented gentlemen from the entertainment department came to the rescue. These guys built and installed all of this in just three days. They did a hell of a job and I believe they deserve a big round of applause. Come on guys, stand up and show my friends who you are."

We felt like big shots. We stood up and bowed to the crowd, then took our seats as the applause grew louder. It felt great, not only because recognition for a job well done is a very pleasant feeling, but also because it's always neat to know people genuinely appreciate the effort that went into your work.

That was a special night I'll never forget. Our women experienced a fantastic evening and we came out looking like Big Shots.

CHAPTER 25

CURTAIN CALL

Being a head carpenter for special events within the Trop has always been enjoyable to me. Every show is different, with different requirements. Also, it's a trouble-shooting kind of job. Little problems arise during the setups and it's my responsibility to make sure they don't become big problems.

When I set up a show, I like to take a couple of minutes to walk around the room and visualize what I'm about to do. I've found that it pays to check with hotel porters just to make sure that we both agree on stage location, location of electricity and sound platforms in the room, and so on. I find out the times other crews are scheduled to work so we don't get in each other's way. I consider many other things which have taken me over twenty-plus years to learn.

After telling you all this, I'll also tell you that sometimes things just happen. Not only that, but many times it's a simple detail that has been overlooked, a thing you'd bet your paycheck would never be a problem. Which brings us to this next little story.

A client brought a show to our convention area one day and, as stage setups go, it was pretty average. The stage was fairly large, with black velour curtains from wall to wall behind the stage.

When the average person sees curtains and staging, he or she takes it for granted, never giving a second thought to the work involved. The show went in very smoothly and we were done well ahead of schedule.

"Dressing out the stage" is a term used when everything is built and the show is ready to go. At this point, we go around and make sure everything looks neat and proper, including the curtains. Many times the curtains will go up first, and they can come in almost any size. The ones I most commonly deal with are sixteen feet high and about seven feet wide. What usually happens is that the stage crew will need to go through the curtains many times during the setup. As a result, we pin them open until right before the doors are opened for the show. At that time someone will go around and close everything up.

Like every other show in the past, spaces were left open, but on the very end of the stage left curtain, the very last panel, a little six-inch piece of curtain came loose and sort of flopped over. The curtains are held in place with Velcro. A piece of wood called a batten has one part of Velcro on it. The opposite piece of Velcro required to make the system work is fastened to the curtain. When you press the curtain to the batten, they stick together. Our curtains overlap, using Velcro once again, so basically each piece of curtain is connected to the piece next to it, essentially becoming one long length of curtain.

Now if you'll remember, that little flap at the end of the curtain is an example of a small detail overlooked. At the end next to the wall, no one in the audience would have ever seen it, but one person who did was a guy employed by the entertainment department who had been asked to come over to the convention area and act as an announcer for the show. All he was going to do was introduce the president of the company to the audience, then leave. Not a stagehand, but rather a management person, he nonetheless possessed a critical eye where stage work was concerned.

With five minutes to kill before the show started, he decided this flaw in the curtain needed to be dealt with and that he was just the guy to do it. There was nothing around that was long enough to reach the top of the curtain. If there had been, he could have used it to press the curtain to the batten. However, another idea popped into his head: if he could grab the end of the curtain and whip it hard enough, with a little luck maybe he could get the top to come together.

His first attempt looked promising, not quite hard enough; he needed to back up a little farther, then whip it forward again. It should work this time. Damn, it touched for just a second. Just a little harder.

But it didn't work. In fact, what happened next was probably his worst nightmare. As he pulled back the curtain, he did it a little harder than he meant to. He heard a sound like material ripping, which was actually the Velcro pieces beginning to separate from each other. He was pretty new to the stage business but he had been around long enough to recognize that sound. With the curtain still clutched in his hand, he stood dead still and for a second all was quiet. Just as he let out his breath in great relief, that slow tearing sound started up again.

Glancing back up at the curtain, he saw it start to peel away from the batten; slowly at first, then all of a sudden it picked up speed. The first panel had now come off the batten and because they were connected, the second panel was now coming down. With the added weight, well, nothing in the world could stop it now.

With a terrible sinking feeling in the pit of his stomach, he watched panel after panel come tumbling down to the ground. With a horrified look on his face, he stood there. He was now looking back at a roomful of people, the end of the curtain still in his hand. He had just pulled down sixty feet of curtain; from the center of the stage all the way to the wall it was now on the ground. Everything backstage was exposed: equipment tables, rear screen projectors, the crew, even the president waiting to go on stage.

It just doesn't get any worse than that, folks. I talked to the sound man, who was sitting at his board out in the audience; he told me that one minute everything was beautiful and the next minute it looked like the whole stage was falling down. Then he noticed one man way off to the side, still holding a piece of curtain in his hand, and he looked like he was going to have a heart attack.

There was only one thing that day which was more incredible than that incident. The convention area can be divided into sections by using what are called air walls, and one of these air walls just happened to be standing two feet in front of where the curtain had been. So a quick-thinking stagehand grabbed a partner and together they pulled the air wall out until it covered one side of the stage. It looked like hell but it saved the day.

Whenever the guys would see this gentleman from management coming around after that, they'd run over to the nearest curtain and pretend to shoo him away, but I'll bet he never thought it was very funny.

CHAPTER 26

IT'S WHO YOU KNOW

Due to the fast pace of our show, the wardrobe department has a couple of quick-change areas on our side of the stage. The wardrobe department in our hotel is made up strictly of women, and they're a real hard working group of people. If the truth be told, they work much harder than I do, and it's unfair that the wage they make is far inferior to stagehands' wages. I hope that one day in the future this situation will be corrected.

Anyway, I really like and respect these gals, but more than that, they all have a great sense of humor and over the years we've had a lot of laughs. There are a couple of women in particular who are…feisty would be a good word, and one in particular, who has been around the business as long as I have, is one of the few people onstage who can really get me going. I kept telling Diane that before I finished writing this manuscript that she'd be in it. Diane kept telling me she'd sue me. Fine. I won't use your name, but I think this little story is kind of funny.

Years ago my wife worked at the Hilton Hotel in the security department. She became very good friends with a gentleman named Dave H., who was also her supervisor at the time. As things happen, my wife left the position, Dave left, and years later Dave showed up at the Trop. Within a couple of years he became Director of Security and let me tell you, he's one of the nicest men I've ever had the pleasure to meet.

So Dave and I run into each other quite a bit. Now it just so happens that Diane has a son named Rick, who has also been at the Trop for quite a few years. Not as long as myself, but over ten years. Rich is also in the security department, a supervisor, and come to find out, is highly regarded by Dave, so much so that Dave considers Rick his second son. All of this I was completely unaware of.

And what's really strange is that I see Rick down in the employee's cafeteria two or three times a week, and have for years. Obviously we're not the best of friends but our relationship over the years has been very cordial. So it's pretty amazing that I never knew his mother was Diane.

One night we were sitting backstage and Diane mentioned the fact that she was going to the "Employee of the Year" dinner and awards ceremony. I said, "You must have been invited because with your cranky old disposition you'd never be nominated in a thousand years."

"Yeah, well Mr. Know-Nothing, it just so happens that the Director of Security, Mr. Hall, has invited me to sit at his table. So there," Diane told me.

"Well Miss Social who got lucky and snagged a free meal, it just so happens that I myself have been acquainted with Mr. Hall over the space of quite a few years and, in fact, we happen to be this close." To show her how close, I held up two crossed fingers. "So I could also sit at his table if I'd wanted to. So there, ha ha. And not only that, if you don't change that snide little attitude of yours, I'll talk to Mr. Hall and you'll be lucky to be able to empty their ashtrays, so you just better be careful, Missy."

"Is that so," Diane said. "Well now, I'm gonna have to talk to Dave and see just how well you two know each other, because I think you're handing me a line of B.S."

It never even crossed my mind to ask her why she was going to the awards banquet in the first place. Diane was going because her son Rick was in the running for "Supervisor of the Year", nominated by Dave, no less, so Mama was invited. You know, I think she did an excellent job at playing dumb because she really got me later.

The evening after the awards Diane came up to me and said, "I spent the whole evening with Dave and he said he barely knows you. Said your wife was one of the nicest people on the planet, but you—he said he'd probably recognize you if he saw you, but close?" She held up her crossed fingers. "Not that close at all."

"Well I'm sure, what with your mouth running all night, it was probably hard for him to concentrate. More than likely you affected his memory, too. You know," I bragged, "Dave isn't my only really good friend in Security; me and a couple of those guys go way back. Why, they never bother me when I park behind the stage doors."

This is a marked No Parking zone where, almost every time I've parked there, I've received a "No Parking Warning Notice" on my windshield. I once got a stern scolding when Security saw me park illegally, then get out and slip an old Warning Notice, which I'd gotten months ago, on my windshield. They said even though the act did exhibit a sense of humor on one level, it was still not a nice thing to do and they weren't that dumb.

I was on a roll now. "Yeah, when they see me come out of the cafeteria with a drink or a sandwich, they just look the other way. My pals."

Diane said, "Well, I know Rick, the evening shift Supervisor, pretty well."

"Yeah, so do I; Rick and I eat together all the time." This was a bold lie. We've always said hello, but in all these years, never once have we sat down and dined together. "As a matter of fact, when I want to take some food out he'll say, 'Phil, let me carry that out for you so you don't get in any trouble.' My old buddy Rick, yeah, we're tight. If ever I have a problem, I go to my best friend Rick," I said.

Diane, God love her, not only let me put my foot in my mouth, but she let me go on until it came out my ass. Then she lowered the hammer.

"Now Phil, are you sure you're telling me the truth? Maybe you're fibbing. Maybe stretching the truth just a tad, huh?"

"Oh good, that's a good one, me stretch the truth—I would never do that. It sounds to me like you're a little jealous of my vast number of acquaintances within the hotel. Well, if you stick around as long as I have, maybe I'll introduce you to some of the higher-ups around here, okay?"

"Okay you ass," she said. "So you say Rick is also one of your best buddies, huh? Well, when he was over for dinner the other night it took me about fifteen minutes of describing your looks, where you worked, how long you worked here, and everything else I could tell him before he finally said, 'Yes, I'm pretty sure I know who he is now.' If he's one of your best friends, I pity you. Also, he said he would never break any rules at the Tropicana. He's expected to set a good example, considering his position, and he would never do something for someone else if it broke the rules.

"By the way, he said he'd better not see you stealing any food. Also, I gave him your car description and license number so they could easily see if you're parked in the wrong spot."

"Wow," I told her. "You sure are a vindictive old woman. Like I'm sure my buddy Rick was over at your house for dinner. Oh I know, he volunteers for the Meals on Wheels senior program; he must have brought you dinner."

All she said was "Look at this, Dumbo." With that, she held out a photo which showed her and Rick in a hug, both smiling. "My husband took that picture on Christmas. That's me and my son, Rick."

Shit!

I learned early on in life that when you are hopelessly busted, the best thing to do is come completely clean. "What a fine looking boy he is; you don't know how many times I've thought that," I said. "Polite as hell, too. You did a fine job raising that one."

"You big bag of B.S., you are truly full of crap, but I got you good this time, you big mouth. I hope you learned something from this little lesson," she said.

"Oh, I did," I said. "I learned that I've let my lying skills really go to the dogs. I'd better practice so next time I won't be so embarrASSed, short for 'not be such an ass.' Thank you very much for the lesson."

On one other occasion—it was a Monday evening, Diane's night off, because it seemed unusually quiet—I asked Sandra, Diane's assistant head of the department, where was the loudmouth this evening?

"Oh, she's off tonight, why?" Sandra asked.

"Because," I said, "It's so nice and quiet back here; none of that usual noise that hurts my ears so much. It's almost eerie."

Sandra, being the polite person she is, told me, "That's not nice; she's a boss and she's a good boss."

Okay, I'm just kidding; besides, if Diane were to get mad at me she might not feed me any more. She just happens to be a fantastic cook; she's made me her special sandwiches on several occasions and someone pointed out to me that I become very possessive of my food, a polite way of saying I don't share.

Anyway, the following evening Diane came up to me and said, "I heard you were running your mouth again when I was off last night."

With the best imitation of a wounded look that I could conjure up I said, "Now Diane, I would never talk about you behind your back. Why, that would be just plain bad manners, and I wasn't raised that way."

"Philip, you are so full of crap it's not even funny. My girls told me what you said, and I quote: 'It's sure quiet back here tonight, I guess the old bag is off, huh?'"

"Whoa, whoa, whoa, wait a minute," I said. "I've been falsely quoted; that's not what I said. Actually I asked where the loudmouth was."

For an old lady she sure does move fast. I was too slow to dodge the box of Kleenex that smacked me in the back of the head, but that was better than a shoe or something else.

She was mad at me for close to a week that time. I would get her so mad at me because I'd go up to her, hold both arms out and motion to her to give me a great big hug. I'd say, "I'm sorry, I feel so bad when you're mad at me. Even though you hate me, I love you." Then I would start to sing the Barney (big purple dinosaur) song. "I love you, you love me…

"Do you want the biggest, swiftest kick in the nuts you could ever imagine? Get away mister; I don't like you. You're lazy. You're all lazy, and you read too much. You're about as useless as tits on a bull!"

Hey, I love you too.

Diane has helped me get through many a boring evening and for that alone, she has my deepest gratitude.

CHAPTER 27

THAT'S ONE BUTT-UGLY PICTURE

When a person is involved with a job that is of a repetitious nature, two things happen.

First is that one becomes so embedded in the same routine that, after a while, it's easy not to pay full attention to the show. It happens to everyone sooner or later. You'll be reading, writing or playing cards when all of a sudden you'll hear a certain piece of music which to you means that you have a cue to do, but suddenly, for the life of you, it's just impossible to remember what exactly your cue is. Most times, if you ask one of the guys around you for help, they can tell you what to do. However, sometimes even they can't help you out because they're concentrating on what they have to do. I've seen times when one guy gets lost, then he gets the guy next to him confused also, and soon it's a chain reaction and everybody's messed up. It's when some of the worst mistakes I've ever seen take place.

Second thing is that the boredom sets in. Every four years or so, we perform what's called a show change. The purpose of this is not only to upgrade the show but also to put in new numbers and scenery, in hopes of keeping the public's interest alive.

It's probably the main reason that so many of the incidents which I've written about happened in the first place. But when things get boring, that's when we get the most creative. Usually it's the things that happen on the spur of the moment that prove to be the funniest.

For example, a while back, one of the girl dancers was leaving our show to dance somewhere else, so on her last night she brought in her camera. She wanted to take pictures of all her friends, plus she wanted some pictures of her dancing onstage.

About midway through the show she came running over to the rail, thrust her camera into the hands of a crewmember and said, "Please hold this for me, I'm almost late for this number. When it's over I'll come back and get it. Thanks."

It's a time-honored tradition on the rail that whenever this particular situation presents itself, that is, any camera is left in our care, this automatically gives us the right to take a couple of pictures of anything we want. This time my boss, who is also named Phil, and myself decided that the girl, whom we'd known for quite a few years, possessed a good sense of humor so we'd provide her with a couple of "special pictures."

Tom, another flyman, was chosen to take the pictures while Phil and I quickly took our pants down, turned our naked butts to the camera and put everything we had into a "moon shot." Gosh, by now we could have posed professionally, as many times as we've done this in the past.

Well, what we didn't count on was Tom's natural God-given talent as a photographer. Also, I believe that the camera was of good quality. The lighting was just right and we did pose for a little longer than normal, because Tom told us he might have messed up when he took the first shot.

It occurred to Phil and me later that Tom didn't actually mess up the first time; he was actually taking the time to really focus in on our butts. Not only that, the second picture he took was such that Tom must have knelt down and in doing this he also got a nice shot of our balls, too.

Not to get off track, but I'm one of those guys whose balls are always in a condition which would lead one to believe that I just climbed out of a freezing lake or something. Get my meaning? On the other hand Phil is, how should I say it? Well, his almost touched his kneecaps when in a bent-over position (his nuts, that is). By the way, when I described mine, I want to make it clear I wasn't referring to my, you know, manhood.

As soon as Tom said he was finished, we all started to crack up. We were trying to visualize just how our friend would find these special pictures. In fact, we weren't all that sure if the people developing them would even give them to her. Perhaps she would be sitting at home with her parents or friends and say, "I just got my pictures back that I took my last night at the Trop. Let's look at them. Oh, here I am with my best friend So and So, and here I am dancing onstage, and here… what the hell…oh my God, oh my God, I don't know how those got in there. Oh my, this is really embarrassing. Shame on those dirty little stagehands.

However it worked out we were pretty sure the joke would be on her. Yes sir, we laughed about the picture taking for quite a few days.

About two weeks later one stage right prop man came over to the rail and said, "There is the most disgusting picture posted on the bulletin board and it's clear that it was taken over here on the rail. It's bad, you gotta see it."

Phil and I both looked at each other and muttered the same word: "Shit." Phil hurried over to the board but I took my time because I had the feeling that this was going to be embarrassing as all hell. I wasn't wrong.

Either she or, well it didn't matter who, but someone had taken one of the photos and had it enlarged. Then they'd gone and made copies on a copy machine, at which time they enlarged the photo even more. Of course by now all the cast and crew had seen the picture, and I later came to find out that it was semi-popular to the point that copies were hanging on all the boys' dressing rooms and they were having quite a time writing little remarks in the space below the photo.

The picture on the main board was special. You know, the butt can really be an ugly sight, especially with you-know-what just hanging down below like a bad dream.

Someone had taken a red marker and made a circle with a line drawn through it like a "no smoking" sign, right on top of Phil's (my boss) butt, with a caption below that said, "Much too hairy, you need to shave that thing." Under mine they wrote something like, "Give that thing a face lift." Now that could really hurt a guy's feelings.

I intended to take the picture down but Phil beat me to it; however, it made no difference because no sooner was it down than another photo would appear. Talk about a joke gone sour. It's amazing these copies didn't show up in other places around the hotel. In the end, even though the joke was on us, we still got quite a laugh over the deal. But next time, and there will be a next time, I believe I'll turn down the modeling job, because a girl's got to protect her reputation, right? Right.

CHAPTER 28

MY AFRICAN PRINCE

One of the gentlemen on my crew goes by the name of Juleik. As you may have guessed by the title, he's a black man. And if my description and terminology is politically incorrect, tough beans.

Juleik is an easy-going fellow, and if rumors are based on fact, he's somewhat of a chick magnet. The good thing about him is that he rarely makes a mistake, which is the main reason I've placed him on the most difficult set of cues. He probably thinks that he's there because I want to make things tough for him. I wouldn't want him to get a big head so I'll just let him think what he wants.

With his relaxed attitude and a natural gift for gab, he's pretty much acquainted with all the cast and crew.

Tyrone, a dancer and over-all character, was talking with Juleik one evening just before the show was ready to start. At "five minutes" (a reminder for cast and crew to get near their positions) the backstage lights are turned off, which left Juleik and Tyrone in the dark, standing behind a curtain.

I was walking over to the rail and when I was almost to the end of the stage I heard these voices. Because it was dark, I slowed down so I wouldn't run into somebody, and that's when I overheard part of the conversation.

Tyrone: "Me too, I just love to dance. I go to all the clubs. Usually a bunch of us go, so you ought to join us some time."

Juleik: "I was just at the Hard Rock last night just kicking it, met some women, hung out all night."

Tyrone: "No kidding, I go there all the time, too."

This went on for a couple of minutes; then the show started and we all went to work.

Always looking for some kind of trouble to get into, it didn't take me long before my huge brain was presented with an idea. I began to wonder how Juleik would respond to a note in which Tyrone would express his desires and fantasies, but because of his shyness, a note was his only option.

Now it's important for you to understand that I know both these guys quite well, and if I though for one second that this little prank would cause any bad feelings or any, say, violent reactions, I would never have done this. Plus, I made sure that I could end this little joke and set the record straight at the first sign of disaster.

Actually it was a little scary how easily the words went onto the paper. Now, I'm not gay but probably because I've worked so long around gay men, subconsciously I know all the lingo—that's it, I swear. This is pretty much the gist of the note:

Dear Juleik,

This is a difficult thing for me to do. I'm so shy that I just couldn't say these things to you so I hope you don't mind that I wrote you this little note.

I really enjoyed talking with you earlier; it seems like we have so much in common that it just freaks me out.

Oh, I'm so nervous I can hardly think, my hands are all shaky, but not as bad as my legs are when I think of you. There, I said it, now before you get all upset, just hear me out, okay?

You are one handsome stud. If you think I'm kidding just check out how the girls all look at you, ooh, I get so jealous I could just scratch their eyes out, the hoochies.

Have you ever had a man before? Have you even thought about it? Oh you don't know what you're missing. When I think about all the things I could teach you, my African Prince, well it just makes my whole body quiver.

When I see you, I just want to eat you up, Cheesecake. That's what you remind me off. Could I call you Cheesecake if no one else is around? Yum, yum, I'm starving already.

I don't want to get too serious here, but if you could just give me a chance, you'd never go back to those dumb broads again.

Before I completely scare you away, please, please don't pay any mind to those silly rumors concerning the size of my manhood. Thirteen inches is just a gross exaggeration. I barely top the tape at ten and a half, and it's not eight inches around, either. I can easily hold it in both hands. However, I hope what I hear about you is true, because any more than a mouthful is a waste.

My goodness, I've said way too much, my little Cheesecake. Don't be shy, let me rock your world. If you're like me and you're too shy to say how you really feel, or if you're confused and you want to try something new, don't forget about me. Just write me a little note; I'll be waiting on pins and needles.

Love Ya,
Tyrone

I folded up the note and shoved it into one of Juleik's gloves; then I told the rest of the guys what I'd done and told them to watch him when he was getting close to doing his first cue.

The show began and I had to avoid Juleik until after he'd found and read the note. If he saw me he'd know I'd done something fishy.

Like the rest of us, Juleik waits to the last second before walking down rail, putting on his gloves and doing his cue. This time Juleik got the first glove on but he was having trouble with the other glove. He finally pulled out some paper that some idiot had shoved in his glove, and just barely did his cue. I was standing a few feet away when I heard one of the guys ask Juleik what was stuck in his glove.

"Hell if I know," he said as he bent over to pick up the paper. He opened it, scanned it for just a second. His face tensed up; then he walked all the way down rail. He sat down and now that he was semi-secluded, he opened the note again and began to read it with what could only be described as concern on his face.

By now we were all watching him and I told the guys that if he looked up and saw us all staring at him, he'd figure it out right away. Everyone did their best to be inconspicuous. Sure enough, after a minute or so Juleik looked around to see if anyone was laughing at him or looked guilty in any way.

He went back to reading the note. He would shake his head as if his mind was overwhelmed with all that it was having to deal with. He set the note down, then almost immediately picked it back up and read some more.

Is it possible for a black man to blush? I don't know, but his face pretty much revealed what his thoughts were concerning any possible relationship with Tyrone, or any man for that matter. He looked like a person who was expecting to bite into a sweet, ripe peach, only to discover it was actually a rotten lemon.

Once again someone asked Juleik what he was reading. Hey, if it was something funny, could he read it after Juleik was finished?

Juleik looked all flustered, lost for words. He just shook his head "no" and put it safely away in his pocket. I was starting to actually feel uncomfortable. I mean, hey, what if Juleik confesses to Tyrone a deep hidden desire to experience the forbidden act of sex with another man, or maybe just a little oral between two friends. Wouldn't really mean that he's gay, but rather a liberated man of the 90's.

I'm just kidding. Anyone who knows Juleik had to figure that right about now he was asking himself what exactly he had done, or what could he have possibly said, that would make Tyrone think he was minutely interested in any affair, or any sex act at all. He was definitely perplexed. Just how would he even be able to discuss this with anyone without being called a fag?

I decided he'd suffered enough. Also, I wanted to end this before they had a chance to run into each other again. Standing next to Juleik, waiting for another cue, I said in a low voice, "Oh, Cheesecake, I could just eat you up"

He started laughing, really hard, and then he said, "You're not very nice. Man, I just couldn't believe it. I mean, we've never had more than a casual conversation and the next thing I know we've got so much in common. All the info about his cock size was scary, but when I think it can't get any worse, it does, because he wants me to give him one chance to fuck me. I know how to let a girl down gently, but how was I going to tell this guy that the only way he'd ever fuck me is if I were dead? Christ, he wouldn't do that, would he?"

"Do what?" I asked.

"You know, that dead thing."

"Gee, I don't know, my African Prince. Hey, why don't we ask him?" I replied.

"You know what, you really are a jerk."

Thank you.

CHAPTER 29

JUST SAY "NO"

Drugs—God, I've done my share, probably did your share too, but even in my most inebriated condition, I still couldn't be put in the same class as some people I know. We had this one guy that did something here at work one night that was so bizarre it's worth writing about.

This guy was big, six feet, five inches tall, extremely strong, and he just happened to be black. I'm not saying this to single out any specific color or ethnic background; it's just that it does have some bearing in regard to this particular story. His name's not important but I'll give you a little background on this fellow.

I'd known him for quite a few years; in fact, we were acquainted well before we both entered into the stagehand business. We both had been stoned together a couple of times and he always seemed to handle himself pretty well.

But there were other times when he would do bizarre things. He told me that he loved to smoke PCP. He also told me that PCP made him uncontrollable at times. For example, he told me about the time he'd smoked quite a bit of it and then had to go home. Driving along the freeway, he decided he had to stop as he was feeling very confined in the car and needed to get out and walk around for a minute. After he pulled over to the side of the road, he hopped out of the car and walked down the road a ways. Already he was feeling better; walking felt good. It occurred to him that if he just took his shirt off, the cool breeze would feel so good on his chest, so nice and cool.

Maybe if he took his pants off he wouldn't feel so restricted; the pants were making him feel so hot. "There, that feels much better; it's amazing, without my pants I can walk so much faster." Can you see where this is going? In no time at all he'd taken all his clothes off and was running along the side of the freeway.

It took a good fifteen minutes for the Highway Patrol to respond. That's not bad, considering this is back when there were no cell phones, and once they'd received the call they were given only an approximate location. From that information, they then had to locate him. Actually it wasn't too hard to spot a six-foot, five-inch, two hundred and sixty pound naked black man running along the freeway. It took a little more time to get additional officers to respond. Finally the police decided their small army of men could now apprehend this psychotic individual.

By the time my friend had begun to slow down, he'd run a little under two miles and his feet were feeling kind of sore. Something was happening up ahead on the freeway; he couldn't really see anything yet, but he knew there was a problem, because there sure were a lot of cops driving by with their lights flashing and sirens blaring. Shit, maybe he was in danger! Maybe he'd better find a safe place to hide. Right now he was in an open area and had no cover.

He ran over to the concrete embankment, jumped over the side and crouched down. Slowly he peeked his head over the top, just a quick glance to make sure nobody was after him. If everything was all right he'd just hide there for a while until the danger passed.

He peeked over the top of the embankment and was scared half to death. Standing there just on the other side was a man, a man with a gun in his hand, and for a second neither one of them said a word. All sorts of visions ran through his head. "He's just going to start shooting me; wait, before he does that he's going to tell me something like, 'Run, you bastard,' or 'I'm going to blow your god damn head off.'"

But all the man said was, "Hi there." Hi there—what the hell did that mean? Hi there—that was a funny thing for a guy holding a gun to say; in fact, that's downright hilarious. Even though he didn't feel threatened by the guy with the gun, he noticed the guy wasn't laughing either. Didn't he see the humor in the situation?

"How ya doing, big guy. Can you tell me what the problem is?"

"Problem? There's no problem with me, but it looks like something's wrong out there," he said. Right then my friend had a mental spike. He realized suddenly this wasn't just some guy; this man was wearing a uniform. Fuck, he's a cop!

"Son, can you tell me why you don't have any clothes on?"

He looked down at himself and a sliver of fear and confusion soon became a runaway train of panic and total bewilderment. "I…I don't know why, I mean I just started walking…I…I don't know who took my clothes. What's going on? Tell me what the hell is going on?

Fortunately the police handled the situation in a very cool fashion. My friend didn't give them any problems. He was allowed to walk to the police car; while they were talking to him, one of the officers calmly put the handcuffs on him and sat him down in the car, and away to jail he went.

Two or three years later, my friend bounced into the Trop to work for a couple of days. Somehow he ended up with a part time schedule that allowed him to work approximately four days a week. Four a couple of months everything went okay; then, out of the blue, all hell broke loose.

If I'm not mistaken, during that particular edition of the Follies show, we had two specialty acts during the show: Cathy, a magician, did her act fifteen minutes into the show; the other act performed twenty minutes before the end of the show. Cathy was in her late twenties and was a very attractive woman. Her body language sent out a message that said, "I'm sexy but classy." Cathy was a nice person and as far as magicians go, easy to work with.

Before the first show that evening, my friend and another person were sitting at our table playing a game of cards. During the games they played, my friend seemed to be unusually happy, and at the time

I had no idea he was just stoned out of his mind. Sure, he seemed a little strange, but then we all were a little strange.

The show began and after a minute or two the head prop man noticed that somebody on his crew just missed a cue. After a second cue was missed, the head prop man knew someone on his crew was missing and he was positive that he knew who it was. During this time Cathy, who was downstairs doing something, followed her usual schedule, which meant she was going up to her room to change into her costume, do her makeup real fast, then go back downstairs and get ready to go on stage.

Cathy's room upstairs was close to the girls' dressing rooms and usually, during any given time, there were at least a couple of girls around, either changing into their costumes or touching up their hair or makeup. For whatever reason, somebody was always hanging around—that is, except for the few minutes Cathy was in her room. It just so happened that because the show had just begun, every female dancer was on stage and only Cathy was left in the dressing room area.

As she reached her room she was kind of confused. She was sure she'd left her door open. Oh well, no big deal, one of the other girls must have closed it for some reason. She opened the door and started to enter the room, but stopped immediately. The lights were off. This set off little alarms in her head; she was positive she left the lights on.

Cathy hesitated for a second. She couldn't shake that uneasy feeling that something was not right, but she didn't have a lot of time. "Oh, you're just being paranoid; the light's burned out, that's all." She had a lamp sitting on the desk where she would sit and do her makeup. With the door open she could easily see well enough to walk across the room and turn it on, however the lamp didn't seem to be in its usual spot. It looked out of place. Cathy always sat closer to the door but things did not look the same, no problem. Cathy was halfway across the room when suddenly the door slammed shut and she heard the "click" of the door lock being engaged.

Total darkness engulfed her. But that was nothing compared to the fear that threatened to paralyze her heart; she was sure she wouldn't even be able to draw her next breath. She was absolutely frozen to the floor. In the grip of sheer panic, she did the only thing she could do: she stood there, dead still, and waited—for what, she had no idea, but she knew that whatever happened, it was not going to be good.

He heard the music begin, but it just didn't seem very important. Besides, the PCP he'd done before the show was exceptionally good, and the really good stuff made him very horny. Sex right now would be the greatest thing in the world. Lately he'd had his eyes on Cathy. Because he worked that side of the stage, it was his job to set her props up right before she did her act. In fact, he'd been talking with her quite a bit lately and she'd always been very friendly towards him. More than friendly; she was kind of a tease.

He saw her standing offstage talking to another girl. Man, she made him horny; it was almost unbearable. If she'd just let him give it to her one time, she'd be hooked. If she followed her same routine (and why wouldn't she?) it would be a couple more minutes before she headed on up to her dressing room to change her clothes.

Because the girls were dancing on stage, he made his way up to Cathy's room undetected. Once inside, he knew they wouldn't have much time. He quickly took all his clothes off and disabled the light. He wanted to make sure she was well into the room before he sprang his little trap. In the dark, behind the door, he waited, armed with his flashlight. He heard light footsteps in the hallway. It was her. Soon he'd show her what lovemaking was all about.

Cathy's mind screamed at her to do something, anything, and just as she was about to scream, from behind her came a voice. "Hey baby, I've been waiting for you." As she turned toward to the voice a light pierced the blackness and in that light was a face. A wicked grin seemed to be stretched from ear to ear.

Cathy could see just enough to make out the countertop that her lamp sat on. Out of instinct more than decision she lunged for the countertop and flipped the switch on. He was caught off guard for a moment, not expecting the bright light, but now he knew there were no more secrets. His identity had been revealed, not that he wasn't going to do that anyway, but it just happened sooner than he expected. "I'm not gonna hurt you baby, good love could never hurt." He pulled a chair to the center of the room and sat his naked body down. "Come here baby, we don't have a lot of time, so we'd better get down to it."

Cathy was a smart girl. If she could just stall long enough they would come looking for her to see why she was late for her act. She went along with his fantasy, telling him she wasn't sure he'd picked up on her signals. What had taken him so long? She said all the right things.

Suddenly there was a knock on her door. "Cathy, are you okay? You're late."

She screamed, ran to the door, unlocked it, and was out of her room before he could ever get up out of the chair. His big fantasy had just ended.

Security entered Cathy's room, where they found him sitting in the corner. They took him into custody, all very peaceful. He has never returned. Since then I have seen him a couple of times and he told me how very lucky he was. To prove it he showed me a tag: Narcotics Anonymous, clean and sober for nine months. Way to go, buddy, keep it up.

We've all had our demons, but if we can just be survivors, then we can make it a better day for everyone else, just one day at a time.

CHAPTER 30

THE GOOD, THE BAD, AND THE UGLY

I've sworn to tell the truth, the whole truth, and nothing but the truth, so help me God. For years I've been writing short notes or letters to guys at work. Actually it would be more accurate to say I've been writing about the guys at work, which usually happens when a person has made a mistake, or something has happened which causes a humorous situation here on the stage, or is somehow connected to the people I work with.

Every story in this manuscript is absolutely true. Because of the time frame in which these events took place—that is, over the last twenty-five years—it wasn't possible for me to place them in chronological order. Also, in some instances I changed the names of people for reasons I felt were best for all parties concerned. Finally, in order to express the humor and increase the interest for anyone who might express the desire to actually read a portion of this story, I've added a little dramatic background (in other words, added a little flavor—no, not lied, but just made it a little smoother).

But I jumped ahead of myself a little so, wait a minute, I was just about to apologize for being disorganized. But apologize to whom? And if someone is actually reading this, then you'll just have to accept the fact that I'm in the advanced stages of "Stageheimer's Disease", a term that one of my closest friends, Allen D., happened to blurt out one day at work when another fellow did something unusually stupid. I thought it was extremely funny then, and now. I repeat that word in my mind quite often and it makes me think of Al, whose life was tragically cut short by an auto accident. For that one word, which perfectly describes a stagehand's mistakes, I've added Al's name into "The Stagehands Hall of Fame."

Sorry, I did it again…where was I? Oh yeah, it seems as though my writing has served a variety of purposes. The most obvious reason was to heckle my workmates, which I must admit gives me great pleasure. Now mind you, I've been doing this for years, and I'm not sure when my writing became a tool; that's the only word I can think of. By tool I mean after years of making people laugh because of mistakes that were made, an unusual thing happened.

On a stage, like many or maybe all workplaces throughout the world, there is a pecking order. Each department's responsibilities fall on the shoulders of its department head. But even under this working structure (which in this case is a Union), there has to be not only a department head but also a person who deals with management and the other department heads. So, in this respect, it's the Head Carpenter whose status is usually a notch above all other department heads onstage.

One evening the Head Carpenter (this has to be at least ten years ago) called me into his office and, upon my arrival, shut the door. I was thinking, "What did I do now?" Instead, he said he had a favor to ask me.

"I've been reading your stuff for quite a while now and it occurred to me that you possess some talents that you may not be aware of," he said.

"Well, explain them to me would you, because at this point in my life I could certainly use any talents, undiscovered or not."

"You see Phil, I've noticed that when you write, almost everyone to a man enjoys reading your material. In a roundabout way, people can laugh at their mistakes, and it seems to eliminate a good deal of embarrassment on their part for having made a stupid mistake. And so I had a thought, and it's this. The one thing I truly hate to do is to issue a crew member and fellow union brother a warning notice." (A warning notice is a notice of reprimand regarding a person's behavior or job performance. Fist notice can be verbal but usually is written so it can be recorded and put in a personal file. Second warning is almost the same as the first, but now management is keeping track. Third warning notice means counseling is strongly recommended, and/or suspended days off from work. It's your last chance. After that, termination.) "Warning notices are no good; it's bad to get one and it's bad to issue one and creates bad feelings. So I wanted to ask you if you'd be willing to write them for me."

"Gee, thanks a lot," I responded. "Like I'd want to do something foolish like that. Why should I take the heat for a responsibility that belongs to you?"

"No, no, hear me out, okay? I'd give you a real warning slip to fill out; however, you'd fill it out, you know, in your normal fashion, like the other stuff you write. The person getting the notice would see at first it's a real notice but after reading it, he wouldn't be so upset. And I'd keep the copy, but I wouldn't turn it in to be filed."

"But what good would that do?" I asked.

"Well," he said, "They'd realize that it could have been handled in the normal fashion, but instead they can sort of laugh it off, but they'd know that it was a warning nonetheless. And as for me, I wouldn't look like a prick."

"Oh, I don't know that this simple plan will change your image, but sure, anything for you, darling," I said.

So my writing wasn't a total waste and, perhaps, just perhaps, it spared some ill feelings, and maybe even saved a job or two. Who knows?

During the process of writing this—whatever this is, or will be—I've realized that regardless of what I've done or haven't done, I recognize the fact that I'm a very fortunate fellow.

There are numerous references to my drug use throughout these pages. I want it to be perfectly clear that the entertainment industry or the people connected with it were in no way an influence or cause of my many years in which drugs were abused. I just believed that I wasn't hurting anyone and that the drugs were incapable of harming me. The truth, as I understand it today, is that these misconceptions were carefully constructed illusions which allowed me to ignore a concept which scared me to death: I was an addict. Long before I even entered this type of work I was addicted to drugs, and in that state, I also used alcohol to take the edge off the drugs. So for years I was dancing with two devils.

In my forty-seven years of existence upon this planet, thirty-two years were spent in the grip of an active addition. There are many opinions and theories on the subject of addiction. For me, I believe that several things were deeply wrong with me; however, even now I don't quite understand what they were. But I'm learning. And I don't do drugs or drink—twenty-four hours at a time, just for today. Sound familiar? Good, then you know where I'm at today.

Through the trials and tribulations of life, God decided that I would seek recovery and that no matter how hard I tried to destroy my life and hurt those around me, in the end I would seek His presence and even pray for Him to show me how to carry out His will. I'm not trying to come off as some religious giant or a preacher; it's not in me. This just happens to be my personal experience and it's working very well for me, so, like they say, "If it ain't broke…

Many of my friends weren't so lucky. For a few, drugs would be directly related to their deaths. Some would be involved in accidents that claimed their lives. Others just went naturally. One thing is certain, I miss them all.

I've been careful not to write anything derogatory about the Tropicana Hotel or the many other institutions which served as my employers. Not because I fear any possible repercussions for the things I might have said, but because in the twenty-seven years that I've been a stagehand, I've only had one bad experience with an employer, and I was partially at fault.

The Tropicana has been a fantastic place to work. When I came to the Trop, it was a simple dispatch call from the Union to replace a full time employee who needed to be off that one night. I ended up staying for the next twenty-five years. The Entertainment Department (management) and my department head, Dion, were gracious enough to allow me to take leaves of absence whenever a more lucrative opportunity presented itself, such as movie work or a TV series. And I believe that was very unusual because some of those jobs lasted for months.

I've had the good fortune to meet many fascinating people over the years. I couldn't even begin to remember all of them, but in many cases it wasn't as simple as "Nice to meet you" and a handshake. In many cases our interaction was on a daily basis, often for weeks at a time. A few I would even be able to introduce as my friend. But what I thought was so exciting was the different personalities I've encountered.

Playing cards with Rodney Daingerfield and getting a glimpse of the real Rodney, a person with a great sense of humor and day-to-day problems, just like the rest of us. Imagine that.

Or standing offstage, talking with comics like Bob Newhart, Rich Little and Don Rickles, just to name a few. Usually our conversations would last three or four minutes before I would hand them the microphone. They could range from "I don't feel like talking tonight" to "Good evening Mr. Ronzone, how are you this evening? Say, would you like to bring a couple of friends to the show as my guests?" Personalities, emotions, just like us.

Entertainers, especially "headliners", often appear to be mysterious and reclusive. They guard their privacy like a dog guards his bone. It's a shame they're forced to do that, but it comes with fame. And that's what makes people like Lance Burton, World Champion Magician, so very special.

Lance signed a contract with the Folies show and stayed for nine years. Our relationship was casual, but anyone meeting Lance for the first time could tell he is a real gentleman. His career went stellar, to the point where one of the largest and certainly one of the most elegant hotels in Las Vegas built a showroom specifically designed for his needs, all high-tech. You could say it was the house that Lance built.

On my daughter's sixth birthday, a big party had been planned at our home. She had invited quite a few people and had picked out her own invitations, cake, decorations, the whole deal. Two days before her birthday she became ill. She was still too sick to get out of bed the day of the party, and we had to cancel it. Dori was devastated. I felt so bad for her but was helpless to do anything more than console her.

Two weeks later we rescheduled her party at a place called Pistol Pete's. However, much of her excitement was lost when the first party was canceled.

A couple of days before her party I was at work early and ran into Lance backstage. He was working on one of his props, so I asked him if he needed a hand. He said sure, so I picked up some tools and went to work.

We were just talking about everyday, normal stuff when the subject turned to my family. I told Lance about my daughter's misfortune and how I just couldn't seem to get her excitement level up. I told him I'd been racking my brains to come up with something special but I wasn't getting anywhere.

"Do you think she would enjoy seeing any magic? I know some pretty neat things," Lance said.

To say I was surprised is an understatement; I mean, here was a guy who performed six nights a week, did all sorts of promotions during the day, and not only that, was going out of town three or four days a week to work on his first televised magic special. I'm quite sure there were many other things he'd rather be doing on a Saturday afternoon besides performing magic at a pizza joint for thirty screaming little kids. I guess I was wrong.

"Wow, Lance, I'm sure she would. That's extremely gracious of you," I said.

"Kids—I love them. What time and where?"

It was funny, because Lance inquired if I could arrange for the place to allow him to hook up a VCR to one of their large screen TV's. I went over to Pistol Pete's and talked to the manager but he said no, he couldn't allow us to do anything that would disrupt business. He would allow Lance to perform, but he'd have to put us in one of the private party rooms, way in the back.

I told Dori that a friend was going to stop by and had a little surprise for her. I didn't make a big deal of Lance's appearance because at her age maybe she'd rather be running around playing games with her friends than watching a magic show.

The party was in full swing when Lance arrived. He set his things up and I introduced him to the adults, then pizza was served and we gathered all the kids up for lunch. As agreed, I didn't say anything; Lance just began doing his magic. When you put thirty kids together at a party, it's total chaos. They're all yelling and screaming, and for the first minute or so, Lance went unnoticed. But not for long.

One by one the kids became silent, their attention locked onto the magic man. Mouths fell open, eyes were wide in disbelief as Lance showed why he was the best sleight of hand artist in the world.

Pizza sat on their plates getting cold; drinks sat untouched. But what really amazed me was you really could have heard a pin drop. I looked over at my sister, who had been sitting near the back of the room; she was no longer there. When I did see her, she had moved up front with the kids, where she had squeezed into a small space. Her face was beautiful, with the same expression of wonderment that the children had.

I looked around the room and was startled to see that our private room was fast filling up with more kids and adults who weren't on the invited guest list. The audience quickly grew to over a hundred; the room was packed.

I began to get a little nervous as the manager's words ran through my mind. Lance was seriously beginning to interrupt business. As far as not drawing attention—forget it. When Lance would complete a trick, the crowd would scream and holler, and the applause was ear shattering.

Appearing like a bad headache, the manager pressed through the crowd, his head turning this way and that. I knew what he was looking for; or rather, who he was looking for. He stopped and looked at Lance and remained still. He'd forgotten about me for the moment. Just like every person who's ever seen Lance perform, he was swept up in the magic.

Forty-five minutes later, Lance wound up his performance and the place exploded with applause. I could hear my sister say, "No, no, don't stop, please that's not fair."

As Lance was ready to leave (after being mobbed by the crowd, during which the adults pretty much pushed the kids out of the way to meet him), I came up and shook his hand.

"Lance," I said, "I'm in your debt. I've never seen my daughter so happy; everyone so happy, for that matter. I'm really grateful." I'll never forget what he said.

"No Phil, it's I who should thank you. It's the kids who are the magic. I love the kids."

Years later my daughter still says, "Dad, you know my birthday when Lance came? I'll never forget it. I've told my friends that he was there, but some of them don't believe me. But I know. Hey, do you think he would come again?"

Well, I don't know if it would happen again, but I also know he would do it if I asked. That's what friends do.

Friends—what would we do without them? In many respects I feel as though I've lived three lifetimes during my career at the Trop. Some of my friends that no longer work here really haven't left, because now their kids are working with me. Very strange.

"Hey, my dad said to say hello. I'm Rob's son and my dad told me if I needed any help to come and see you." I like that.

People come and go, but it seems that in this business we sort of keep track of one another. As a person who uses people from the Union when needed for special events, or whatever the reason, I have opportunities to stay in touch, meet some of the new members, and hopefully make some new friends.

As a department head you have to do certain things in order to survive. When you've been an assistant in a department, you just do your job and everything will be just fine; however, when they came to me with the offer of Department Head on a fulltime basis, I had some reservations. The guys who were my friends were now also to become my assistants. Something at gut level told me that no matter how hard I tried, our relationship would change. And it did.

Not that it was a bad thing, because it caused me to grow some in the relationship department of my life. That's not to say it was an uncomfortable feeling at times. It seemed that some guys thought I might be more flexible with the rules or that they could relax a little, which means their work ethics became sloppy.

Someone asked me if I felt more powerful as a Department Head, and it was sort of funny that he should ask me that because I'd been thinking about that for a while.

"No, I don't feel any power at all. In fact, I'm feeling just the opposite. Think about it. I'm really at the mercy of my crew. If you guys want to screw me, all you have to do is make mistakes on a consistent basis. Ginny, the Entertainment Director, will say that Phil Ronzone is either unwilling or unable to lead his crew, so he has to go.

Maybe I'm not your vision of a perfect boss but you could do a lot worse; plus, you know what you've got. Now if you guys are the cause of me being replaced and they don't promote from within, who knows what kind of person will be brought in to be your boss," I told him. "You guys take care of me, I'll do my very best to stand behind and take care of you guys."

I have tried to lead my crew by following a few simple rules:

Number one, I never ask anyone to do anything that I wouldn't do myself, ever. If I don't know how to do it, I'll learn. I believe respect is earned by setting a good example, work ethics and attitude, neat and clean appearance.

Number two, don't violate the rules you expect your crew to follow. I can't tell you how many times I've seen this happen, and as an assistant I would think, "What the hell, what makes him exempt? Is it a perk that comes with the position or does he think he's better than the rest of us?" Any way you look at it, violating the very rules you set in place produces negative results.

Number three, I always try to treat the people who work for me as if tomorrow they could be my boss. It's happened before; in fact, my last boss worked for me a number of times in the convention area. His name happens to be Phil also, and his first night on the rail as our Department Head he came up to me and said, "You might not remember me but I've worked for you a couple of times. I remember you."

"Oh boy, I'm in trouble now. Well, please tell me I was nice to you," I said.

"Yes, you were, and if you hadn't been I wouldn't have worked for you again." Thank the good Lord.

Number four, when I act as Head Carpenter for special events and the crew is fairly large, I get all the carpenters together and give them this little speech: "Guys and gals, throughout the day I'll be giving you various jobs to do. Now I realize that there is more than one way to do many of these jobs. You may do these jobs your way as long as they're done in a safe manner and it looks professionally done. The only exception is if I specifically tell you to do it a certain way; it's because I have a reason to.

"The last thing is, if you don't understand what I want done or if you have any questions at all, please ask. It could be something I've overlooked which would be a great help to me. However, if you tell me you understand and then you do it all wrong, I'm gonna get upset with you, and this will ruin both our days."

These simple rules have served me well and I say with pride that over all these years I've never had to terminate one single person, not even give a warning notice.

It's been quite a journey. I thank God that I'm still here to write this. I've been blessed with a wife whom I love and who loves me. She's been my very best friend, though I didn't realize it for many years. She has supported me in every endeavor I've undertaken, and some were disastrous. Not once did I hear, "I told you so." The sad part is that for many years my bad habits affected all areas of our marriage, but she still stayed by my side. It wasn't until recent years, with a clear head, that I recognized that whatever success I have had, I couldn't have done it without her support. I love you Tomijean.

Dori, my daughter—what can I say? A father couldn't be prouder. I brag about her so much at work the guys are probably tired of listening to me. It has bothered me for years that I work at night and I'm not home with her and Tomijean. Because my wife works and my daughter goes to school, our time together is much more limited than your normal family. Dori is a straight-A student taking all accelerated classes, entering her eleventh year of ballet, and also is an honor choir member. What more could a father ask for? Tomijean, who was home with her all those nights, is the one who deserves all the credit. She installed in Dori all the good traits and tools that have allowed her to be so successful in her young life—another thing my wife dedicated herself to.

In closing, I want to pay tribute to several people. These guys are no longer with us but I'll never forget them.

The great Dion, who definitely marched to a different drummer. In fact, it wasn't even a drummer. I asked him why he always gave me so many more jobs to do while the rest of the guys on his crew seemed to be able to relax and not get involved.

Dion told me, "You could have asked, why do I make you do more work? I'll tell you. It's been my experience that the laziest guy on the crew usually finds the easiest way to do things." But you see, that's what I loved about Dion, because from him that was a compliment. If you did something good—say, for instance, you did a cue that someone else missed, or stopped a guy from making a mistake— maybe you'd want the boss to know you did some show-saving action. Most bosses would probably say, "Hey Phil, nice job, thanks." From Dion you'd hear something like, "Hey, you really did that well. That makes me happier than a sissy with two assholes. That's what you're supposed to do, ya dick."

When you hear the term, "He was a man's man," I always think of Dion; it's the perfect description. He taught me that you don't whine; nobody likes a whiner. However, no matter how hard he tried to hide it, his heart of gold would shine through. He loved to build, and I couldn't tell you how many people he helped out when help was desperately needed.

The day Dion passed away was New Year's Eve. Even in his passing, it would be on the most celebrated day of the year. It was also one of the saddest days of my life.

See you around Dion; I miss you, buddy.

Allen D., who sadly was Dion's nephew, also is gone but never forgotten. God, there was no one like him: tough, strong, so very quick with his hands.

For years people talked about three dimensions; once or twice I heard about the fourth dimension, but that was about it. And I'll be the first to tell you my knowledge about such matters is extremely limited.

Allen told me, "You know why anything is possible? When an event happens, and scientists or expert persons say in regard to that event that it's unexplainable or it's not possible, those people are the ones who have set limits in their minds. Or they are people who have put themselves so high up on the intelligence ladder as to be in the same class as the Almighty. Absurd. Don't they realize that there are many dimensions? And who's to say things don't cross over or interfere with one another once in a while? I don't know why they can't figure it out; I can see it so easily in my mind."

He drew fantastic pictures, faces within faces, really dynamic, with order and chaos mixed together. He would explain to me the dimensions and I would fail miserably in understanding what he saw and I couldn't see, but I never doubted him.

Allen found this little camp of homeless guys who lived in the desert. Many times after work he would go out there and spend hours with them. "Phil, did you know that one of those guys out there is a college professor and another one is an architect?" Sometimes he would spend his whole paycheck on food and take it out to them. I would never have known except that one time I helped him take the food out, and I met some of the guys. Everything he told me was true.

I had an Afghan hound dog, very beautiful but very stupid; I don't know, maybe it was the owner. Anyway, Allen and I ate some acid once and we took the dog with us to a place called Calico Basin, about twenty miles out of town.

These dogs are fast. They also possess a coat of long, fine hair, and when all cleaned and brushed, are a beautiful breed of dog. Shawnee, my dog, was mostly white with black patches here and there.

The reason we brought her with us was because this particular evening the moon was bright, and when Shawnee ran around, she looked like a ghost. She would shimmer and glow. It was really awesome. We'd done this before, and Shawnee seemed to love it up there also, so I had no reason to think this time would be any different.

So there we were, feeling pretty messed up, and watching Shawnee run around this huge meadow looking beautiful and mysterious at the same time.

All of a sudden we saw a small glowing thing pop up in front of Shawnee and move off at a high rate of speed. A second later, Shawnee saw it and followed in fast pursuit. Being high on the acid, we thought it was pretty spectacular watching the ghost chase whatever it was across the meadow. Then they reached the end and went down into a little gully and back up the other side.

"Gee," Allen said. "She sure looks beautiful."

"Fast, too," I said.

Down another little gully and up again. Shawnee was now just a small blur.

"Uh, Phil, she'd kind of far away. Maybe we should call her or something."

As it turned out, we chased that dog for hours. To her it was a game; to us the game had been over with hours before. But the funny thing is, it was Allen who physically ran the dog down. And if you know that breed of dog, that was no easy thing.

I've always been a mountain man at heart, but the times I spent in the mountains with Al—well, he was like Grizzly Adams. We were pushing rocks off a cliff one night. We started with small boulders, but they soon became boring. It was about three in the morning; the moon was so bright you could easily see without flashlights. Up on that mountain, all was deathly quiet, until you heard the boulders crashing down.

We became more daring, selecting larger and larger boulders to push off the mountain. Finally, we selected a huge one; it took all our strength to roll it to the cliff edge.

This turned out to be one of those major lessons in life, and this particular lesson was: if you do stupid things, stupid things happen. Sometimes you can get hurt—even killed.

At the last moment, just before we were going to give that boulder our last desperate shove over the cliff edge, my hands slipped. When that happened, Allen lost his grip, too. The boulder was at least four hundred-plus pounds. And as it rocked back to the ground, it came down right against my shin, tearing large strips of skin from my leg and then proceeding to bounce once or twice on my foot.

Now, normally, this is where the average person would insist on going directly to the hospital.

"Oh Christ, Allen, that hurt like a son of a bitch. I'm pretty sure I just broke a couple of toes and my leg is bleeding an awful lot, buddy. We should probably head back into town, maybe drop me off at the emergency room."

"What did you say?" Al looked at me in disbelief. "Are you serious? I'll admit you got a few scrapes on your leg, but hey, you're not a man until you bleed. So come on, suck it up and let's climb the rest of this mountain, you big pussy. Look, the top's just right up there, so let's go."

So we did just that. I sure as hell didn't want to be a pussy. We climbed, we hiked, and climbed a little more and then it was finally time to go home.

"Hey, you're a pretty tough guy; you only cried once. I'm proud of you," Allen said.

Later that morning at the emergency room, the doctor confirmed what I already knew. I had three broken toes, and if you've ever had any, you know there's not a damn thing you can do with them except walk if you have to walk.

But the point is, Allen was a motivator, a do-er; he didn't care much, if anything, about others' opinions. He was on a mission to live life to the fullest. And during the time that I knew him, that's just what he did. If ever there was a guy whom you considered indestructible, Al was that guy.

As I've mentioned, this is a family business. Working within the

Tropicana was Bob, Allen, Jack (their father), Dion (Jack's brother), and Dick (another brother). Quite a few people who were related.

I can remember the time as if it was yesterday, although in reality it's been almost fifteen years. We were putting in a New Year's Show in the convention area, and around 10:30 a.m. there was a telephone call. I knew something was wrong immediately; they asked for Jack or Bob, and since Bob was nearest, I handed him the phone. A couple of words into the conversation, his facial expression had changed to deep, uncomprehending anguish. He kept shaking his head, and then he hung up.

"I need to get Jack and then we both have to go to Jack's house. Allen died about a half hour ago. He was driving down Lake Mead Boulevard; his truck went off the road and flipped a couple of times. He was ejected out of the truck. He was dead when the ambulance arrived."

A part of me died that day also. I went up to the mountains after work that evening, to a spot where Allen and I had been so many times before. I sat all night. I was crying for the longest time, until there were no tears left. Than I was able to laugh, and to remember all we'd done in those years we shared as friends. I was fortunate to have known him, and to this day I can look around this stage and still feel his presence.

Someday, Allen, will you greet me and take my hand, show me all the dimensions, show me all the secrets that you tried to enhance my life with? Just show me everything, okay? Okay.

I have one more person I need to mention. If you're getting bored, tough cookies—this one belongs to me.

Tom R, big Tom, the gentle giant; he could make the sweetest voice come out of that big old body. The man could sing. See, Tom's dream in life, I believe, was to be an actor. Here was another guy who just enjoyed talking to people, helping people—he just loved people. If you wanted to find out what was going on around the hotel, Tom was the guy to talk to, and he seldom revealed his sources.

Here was a guy who visited his parents every day of the year. I always thought that was pretty neat; in fact, in a way, Tom brought me closer to my own parents.

Tom made quite a few commercials for local television and we used to kid him a lot, because a few of them seemed to be on TV all the time. We'd tell him that if we saw them one more time, we'd strangle him.

So many things happened to him—some people are like that, stuff just happens. If a person was going to get injured while we were fooling around, it would be Tom. If we were playing cards for money, Tom would lose. Well, you get the picture. Still, throughout it all, he always kept his sense of humor and that, my friends, is a great, great virtue. There were so many times he'd tell me a joke that would just make my day. He was like a bartender; he had a million jokes.

On his fiftieth birthday, Tom passed away.

I miss the big guy. His passing was sudden and unexpected; it seems like these things usually are. He will not be forgotten.

Well, that's how I remember it. It's kind of sad because I realize that nothing lasts forever, and I'm quite sure I won't be here for another 25 years. The Folies Bergere celebrated forty years of continuous running time, the longest-running show in United States history.

We have quite a few young guys onstage, and it's my opinion that this is a great stage crew. Like all people who work together night after night, we laugh, we fight, and sometimes we even cry together. Most of all we bitch together when new work rules are put into effect. But I remind these guys that they are working on a part of history. They just walked into that; me, I had to be here 25 years to be a part of this. So we have to be the best, all of us.

Now here's the truly amazing thing, and this pertains mainly to the crew. In the 25 years that I've been here, there is not one person, not one, who wasn't a pleasure to work with, and I really, truly mean that. I cannot think of one person who didn't teach me something. And that, I think, is why the years passed so quickly.

I owe thanks to the guys I work with on the rail: Brian, Gabor, Juleick, Mike and Ted. My good friends, the ones who know me the best and still put up with me. At the risk of being called a fag, again, I love you all.

So this comes to an end, for now. If anyone reads this and enjoys it, but you're not a stagehand (oops—shit, I just missed a cue)...Where was I?...Oh yeah, if you enjoyed this but are not a stage hand, well, there is a great chance you should have been one.

Bye Bye,
Phil Ronzone

P.S. Since writing this, one thing has happened that deserves recognition, so here goes. My sister Rhodie undertook the task of editing and printing this whole mess, and sent me the last chapter so I could put the finishing touches together. I was to send it back to her so she could complete her task.

So I bring the last chapter to work and a fellow crewmember by the name of Vance is working the rail that evening. Now Vance is about my age and has been a stagehand as long as I have, so I think, "Hey, maybe Vance would read this chapter and tell me what he thinks of it."

Vance, God bless him, is really anxious to read my work, so I hand it over. This is at the end of the first show. All during the second show Vance is reading. Christ, there wasn't that much to read; oh well, maybe he's a slow reader.

Finally Vance comes back to me ten minutes before the show's over and sits down across from me. His face is serious, like he's pissed off.

"Phil," he says, "you know, I'm very disappointed in you." (All the time he's talking, he's waving my last chapter in front of my face.) "You write this whole damn book, 25 years' worth of stuff and not once, not even one time, did you mention the day that I saved you from that shit-eating dog." And with that, he tore up the whole chapter.

I was stunned, then angry; how could he do that to my work? I was actually speechless, something new to me. I was just about ready to grab him when the slightest smile appeared at the corner of his mouth.

Vance had gone into the office and photocopied the first page, then grabbed a bunch of blank sheets of copy paper. When he put it all together it looked just like my copy.

For just a minute, he had me good. But that's what it's all been about. Good, healthy fun—may that never end.

Philip Ronzone
ronzonephilip@gmail.com

PROLOGUE

Thank God that I was somehow led to union Local #720 in Las Vegas, Nevada. I knew nothing about being a stagehand. If not for the union, my life would have been much different.

I believe unions are good. However some would argue that unions are not so good.

Some people even describe unions as evil. To those people I would say that if unions are evil, it is a necessary evil. People don't realize that unions, of, past, were the foundation and benchmark for many good paying jobs outside of a union's jurisdiction. In other words, unions have influenced many positive aspects for the working men and women who normally could be treated unfairly by employees who simply do not care for the welfare of their employees.

It is very important that I acknowledge my union, Local#720, for the opportunity to earn a very good living. I had job security, excellent healthcare and insurance provided to me. Not to mention the retirement pension which allows my wife and I to live very comfortably.

Printed in the United States
By Bookmasters